MEN IN WHITE

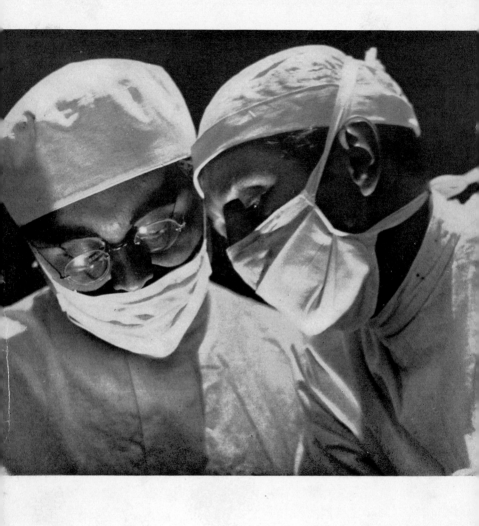

Sidney Kingsley

MEN
IN
WHITE

A Play

IN THREE ACTS

COVICI · FRIEDE, PUBLISHERS

NEW YORK

DEDICATION

TO THE MEN IN MEDICINE

WHO DEDICATE THEMSELVES,

WITH QUIET HEROISM,

TO MAN.

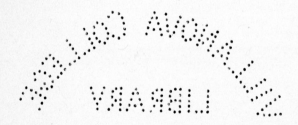

"I swear by Apollo, the physician, and Aesculapius, and Hygieia, and Panacea and all the gods and all the goddesses—and make them my judges—that this mine oath and this my written engagement I will fulfill as far as power and discernment shall be mine. . . .

"I will carry out regimen for the benefit of the sick, and I will keep them from harm and wrong. To none will I give a deadly drug even if solicited, nor offer counsel to such an end; but guiltless and hallowed will I keep my life and mine art.

"Into whatsoever houses I shall enter I will work for the benefit of the sick, holding aloof from all voluntary wrong and corruption. Whatsoever in my practice, or not in my practice, I shall see or hear amid the lives of men which ought not to be noised abroad—as to this I will keep silent, holding such things unfitting to be spoken.

"And now, if I shall fulfill this oath and break it not, may the fruits of art and life be mine, may I be honored of all men for all time; the opposite if I transgress and be foresworn."

—Excerpts from the Hippocratic oath, to which physicians have bound themselves since the days of antique Greece.

PERSONS IN THE PLAY

ON THE STAFF OF ST. GEORGE'S HOSPITAL

DR. GORDON	*Attending in Medicine*
DR. HOCHBERG	*Attending Chief of Surgical Staff*
DR. MICHAELSON	*Interne*
DR. VITALE	*Young Practitioner*
DR. MC CABE	*Retired Surgeon*
DR. FERGUSON	*Interne, House Surgeon*
DR. WREN	*Attending in Medicine*
DR. OTIS ("SHORTY")	*Interne*
DR. BRADLEY ("PETE")	*Interne*
DR. CRAWFORD ("MAC")	*Interne*
BARBARA DENNIN	*Student Nurse*
NURSE JAMISON	
NURSE MARY RYAN	
FIRST NURSE	
SECOND NURSE	
ORDERLY	

OTHER CHARACTERS

MR. HUDSON	*A Wealthy Patient*
JAMES MOONEY	*His Business Associate*
LAURA HUDSON	*His Daughter*

DR. LEVINE	*In General Practice*
DR. CUNNINGHAM	*A "Courtesy" Physician at St. George's*
DOROTHY SMITH	*A Young Patient*
MRS. SMITH	*Her Mother*
MR. SMITH	*Her Father*
MR. HOUGHTON	*A Trustee of the Hospital*
MR. SPENCER	*A Trustee of the Hospital*
MR. RUMMOND	*A Trustee of the Hospital*
MRS. D'ANDREA	*The Mother of a Patient*

The entire action takes place within the walls of St. George's Hospital.

Photograph for the frontispiece by Alfredo Valente, by courtesy of *The Stage*.

All other photographs of the original stage production, including that used on the jacket, by Vandamm Studio.

ACT ONE

Scene 1

THE *library of St. George's Hospital. The staff of the hospital gather here to read, to smoke, and to discuss many things—primarily Medicine.*

This is a large, comfortable room flanked on the left by tall windows, on the right by ceiling-high bookcases crammed with heavy tomes. There is a bulletin-board in one corner, on which various notices, announcements, advertisements, schedules, etc., are tacked; there is a long table, an abandon of professional magazines and pamphlets strewn upon it; there are many plump leather club chairs, some of which are occupied at the moment by members of the staff. In a series of stalls against the back wall are a number of phones.

Niched high in the wall is a marble bust of Hippocrates,[1] the father of Medicine, his kindly, brooding spirit looking down upon the scene. At the base of the bust is engraved a quotation from his Precepts: *"Where the love of man is, there also is the love of the art of healing."*

---

[1] *Hippocrates* (460 to 359 B.C.): ancient Greek physician whose figure is revered by all medical men as that of the ideal physician. He has left a group of writings known as the "Hippocratic Collection", and an oath which is the beacon for all ages of the incorruptibility of medicine.

A number of the staff are smoking and chatting in small groups, the nucleus of each group being an older man in civilian clothes—an attending physician; the young men, internes, recognizable by their white short-sleeved summer uniforms, are doing most of the listening, the older ones most of the talking, the hush of the room on their voices.

One elderly white-haired physician, seated well to the right, is straining his eyes over a thick medical volume. A number of other books and pamphlets are on a stool beside him. A middle-aged physician, his back to us, is searching the bookcase for a desired volume. A younger practitioner is standing by the window, looking out into the street.

Through a wide, glass-panelled, double door, set in the rear wall, we see a section of the corridor alive with its steady cavalcade of nurses, internes, etc., all hurrying by to their separate tasks. The quick activity of the hospital outside contrasts noticeably with the classical repose of the library.

The loud speaker at the head of the corridor calls: "Dr. Ramsey! Dr. Ramsey! Dr. Ramsey!"

Phone rings. An interne crosses to the phones, picks one up, talks in low tones.

Enter Dr. Hochberg, a short, vital man, whose large head is crowned by a shock of graying hair. He carries himself with quiet, simple dignity. There is strength in the set of his jaw; but the predominating quality expressed

in his face is a sweet compassion—a simple goodness.[1]
That he is a man of importance is at once apparent in the
respectful attention bestowed on him by the others.

DR. GORDON (*the middle-aged physician, who has just*
found his book) *sees Hochberg:* Ah, Doctor Hochberg!
I've been waiting for you. *He quickly replaces the volume*
and goes to Hochberg.

The young practitioner by the window wheels round at
the mention of Hochberg's name.

DR. GORDON: There's a patient I want you to see.

DR. HOCHBERG: Certainly, Josh. We'll look at him in a
minute. I just—— *His eye sweeps the room.* George Ferguson isn't here, is he?

MICHAELSON (*one of the internes seated*) *looks up from*
his reading: No, Dr. Hochberg. Shall I call him?

HOCHBERG *nods:* Please.

Michaelson rises and goes to a telephone.

DR. VITALE (*the young practitioner*) *leaves the window*
and approaches Hochberg: Er . . . Dr. Hochberg——

HOCHBERG: Good morning, doctor.

VITALE: I sent a patient of mine to your clinic yesterday.
Did you have a chance to . . . ?

HOCHBERG *recollecting* Oh—yes, yes. *Reassuringly,*
knowing that this is perhaps Vitale's first private patient,

---

[1] "All knowledge attains its ethical value and its human significance only
by the humane sense in which it is employed. Only a good man can be a
great physician".—Nothnagel.

and most likely a relative at that: No rush to operate there. You try to cure him medically first.

VITALE *relieved:* I see. All right, doctor. Thank you. Thank you.

HOCHBERG: Not at all. Keep in touch with me. Let me know what progress you make.

VITALE: I will.

HOCHBERG: If we have to, we'll operate. But I think if we wait on nature this case will respond to expectant treatment.

VITALE: Right! *He goes.*

GORDON *shakes his head, kidding Hochberg:* Fine surgeon you are—advising against operation!

HOCHBERG *smiles and shrugs his shoulders:* Why not give the patient the benefit of the doubt? You can always operate! That's easy, Josh.

MICHAELSON *returning from the phone:* Dr. Ferguson'll be right down, sir.

HOCHBERG: Thanks.

GORDON: I hear you've some interesting cases at your clinic.

HOCHBERG: Yes, yes—er—suppose you have dinner with me tonight. We'll talk, hm? I discovered a little place on Eighty-fourth Street where they serve the most delicious schnitzel and a glass of beer (*measuring it with his hands*)—that high! . . . But beer!

GORDON: Sounds good. I'll just phone my wife and——

HOCHBERG: It won't upset her plans?

GORDON: Oh, no! *He crosses to the phone.*

HOCHBERG *approaches the white-haired physician and places a hand gently on his shoulder:* And how is Dr. McCabe today?

MC CABE: My eyes are bothering me! *He indicates the pyramid of books beside his chair.* Trying to read all of this new medical literature. It certainly keeps piling up! *He shakes his head.* Has me worried!

HOCHBERG: But, why?

MC CABE *nods toward internes:* These young men today —How can they ever catch up with all this?[1]

HOCHBERG: These young men are all right. They're serious—hard-working boys. I've a lot of faith in them.

MC CABE: But there's so much. *He shakes his head.* We've gone so far since I was a boy.[2] In those days appendicitis was a fatal disease. Today it's nothing. These youngsters take all that for granted. They don't know

---

[1] "The amount of human labor and ingenuity that is now being thrown into the investigation of Nature is almost incredible even to men of science. Some conception of the enormous and unreadable bulk of scientific literature may be gained by a glance at the 'International Catalogue of Scientific Literature'. This gives the *titles alone* of original articles in the various departments of physical science. These titles for the year 1914 alone occupied seventeen closely printed volumes! The rate of publication has accelerated considerably since then. There are very few departments of science which do not have some bearing on Medicine. It is evident that no human mind can possibly compass even a year's output of this material."—Charles Singer in "A Short History of Medicine".

[2] Medicine has advanced farther in the last fifty years than in the preceding fifty centuries.

Without anaesthesia, asepsis and X-ray, all of which were developed during the last half-century, major surgery would have remained an impossible dream.

the men who dreamed and sweated—to give them anaesthesia and sterilization and surgery, and X-ray. All in
my lifetime. I worked with Spencer Wells in London,[1]
and Murphy at Mercy Hospital.[2] Great men. None of
these youngsters will equal them. They can't. There's too
much! I'm afraid it will all end in confusion.

HOCHBERG: Where the sciences *in general* are going to
end, with their mass of detail—nobody knows. But, good
men in medicine . . . we'll always have. Don't worry,
Dr. McCabe . . . one or two of these boys may surprise
you yet, and turn out another Murphy or another Spencer
Wells.

MC CABE *shaking his head:* Not a Spencer Wells! No!
Not a Spencer Wells! *Hochberg helps him rise.* Chilly
in here, isn't it? *He walks slowly to the door.* I'm always
cold these days. *He shakes his head.* Bad circulation!

*Gordon finishes his phone call, hangs up and crosses
to Hochberg.*

HOCHBERG: All right for dinner, Josh?

GORDON: Oh, of course. Certainly!

*An interne, George Ferguson, and an attending physi-
cian, Dr. Wren, come up the corridor engaged in discus-
sion. The interne stops outside the door to give some in-
structions to a passing nurse, who hastens to obey them.*

---

[1] Thomas Spencer Wells (1818-1897): pioneer in abdominal surgery—
noted for his simple and effective methods.
[2] J. B. Murphy (1857-1916): outstanding among the men who developed
the technique of abdominal surgery.

He pauses in the doorway of the library, still talking to Dr. Wren.

George Ferguson is about twenty-eight; handsome in an angular, manly fashion, tall, wiry, broad-shouldered, slightly stooped from bending over books and patients; a fine sensitive face, a bit tightened by strain, eager eyes, an engaging earnestness and a ready boyish grin.

FERGUSON: If we used Dakin tubes [1] it might help. . . .

DR. WREN: They're worth a trial!

FERGUSON: And, this afternoon, first chance I have, I'll take him up to the O.R.[2] and debride all that dead tissue.

WREN: Good idea! *And he marches on down the corridor.*

Dr. McCabe reaches the door. Ferguson holds it open for him. McCabe returns Ferguson's smile and nod. McCabe goes on. Ferguson enters and approaches Hochberg.

MICHAELSON: They've been ringing you here, George.

FERGUSON: Thanks, Mike! *To Dr. Hochberg:* Good morning, Doctor Hochberg.

HOCHBERG: Good morning, George.

FERGUSON: I was down in the record room this morn-

---

[1] Dakin tubes: arrangement of tubes invented during the world war by Dr. H. D. Dakin to provide constant flushing of deep and gangrenous wounds with an effective antiseptic (Dakin's solution) also devised by him.

[2] O.R.: hospital jargon for operating-room.

ing. *He takes a pack of index-cards out of his pocket.* The first forty-five cases seem to bear you out. . . .

HOCHBERG *smiles:* Uh, hm! . . .

FERGUSON: Some three hundred more charts to go through yet, but. . . .

GORDON: What's this?

HOCHBERG: Oh, Ferguson and I are doing a little research. I have some crazy notions about modern surgical technique. Ferguson, here, is writing a paper to prove that I'm right!

FERGUSON: As a matter of fact, Dr. Hochberg is writing the paper. I'm just helping collect the data and arrange it.

HOCHBERG: Ah! You're doing all the hard work! How's 217?

FERGUSON: Pretty restless during the night, but her temperature's down to normal now.

HOCHBERG: Good! And Ward B—bed three?

FERGUSON: Fine! Asked for a drink of whiskey.

HOCHBERG *smiles:* He'll be all right.

FERGUSON: He is all right! *He grins.* I gave him the drink.

HOCHBERG *laughs:* Won't hurt him. . . .

FERGUSON *becomes serious, turns to Dr. Gordon:* I wish you'd have another look at 401, Doctor.

GORDON: Any worse today?

FERGUSON: I'm afraid so. He's putting up a fight, though. He may pull through.

GORDON *shaking his head dubiously:* Mm, I don't know.

FERGUSON: I hope so. He's a fine fellow. He's planning great things for himself—when he gets out of here.

GORDON *significantly: When* he gets out. . . .

The phone rings. A short interne crosses to phones and picks one up.

HOCHBERG: Oh, by the way, George, we're sending Mr. Hudson home Tuesday.

FERGUSON *suddenly excited:* Tuesday? Great! Does Laura know, yet?

HOCHBERG *nods:* I phoned her this morning.

FERGUSON: She happy?

HOCHBERG: Naturally!

FERGUSON: I wish you had let me tell her.

HOCHBERG *twinkling:* Ah—I should have thought of that!

SHORTY *at phone:* One second. *Calls:* Ferguson! For you.

HOCHBERG: Go on! Call for you. *Ferguson goes to phone. Hochberg beams at Gordon.* Good boy! Lots of ability! We're going to be proud of him some day.

Enter a lean, shabby man who at first glance appears out of place here. His coat is rusty, and rough weather has left its stain on the hat he carries so deferentially. Tucked under one arm is a large envelope of the type used for X-ray pictures. He has a timid, beaten manner. He is a fairly young man, but worry has lined his forehead, and prematurely grayed his hair, making him seem years older. He hesitates at Dr. Hochberg's elbow, and finally ventures to touch it.

HOCHBERG *turns, looks at him. Politely, as to a stranger:* Yes? *Suddenly he recognizes the man.* Why . . . Levine! *He grips Levine's arms with both hands, almost in an embrace.* My dear Levine! . . . I didn't recognize you. . . .

LEVINE *nods and smiles sadly:* I know.

HOCHBERG: Dr. Gordon! You remember Dr. Levine?

GORDON *hesitates a moment:* Why, of course. *They shake hands.*

HOCHBERG: Such a stranger! Where have you been hiding all this time? Why it must be . . . five years since. . . .

LEVINE: Six!

HOCHBERG: Six? My! Mm. . . . *To Gordon:* We're getting old. *Then, affectionately:* Ah! It's good to see you again.

LEVINE: It's nice to get back, but. . . . *He looks around.* Things here seem pretty much the same. New faces— that's all.

GORDON: Nothing much changes in a hospital.

LEVINE: Only people! We change . . . get old . . . break up so quickly. *The tragic quality in his voice affects the others. Pause.*

GORDON: Well. . . . *To Hochberg.* I'm going up to look at that boy in 401. *Hochberg nods. Gordon turns to Levine.* I'm glad to have seen you again. *Exit Gordon.*

HOCHBERG: Tell me . . . how are things with you?

LEVINE: Oh. . . . *He shrugs his shoulders.* Just about getting along.

HOCHBERG: And how is Katherine?

LEVINE *his brow wrinkles:* Not so well.

HOCHBERG *concerned:* What seems to be the trouble?

LEVINE: Her lungs. . . . She has a slight persistent cough! Some X-rays [1] here. . . . *He opens the large envelope he is carrying and from it takes two X-ray plates. Hochberg holds up the plates to the window and examines them.*

Ferguson hangs up and returns to Hochberg.

HOCHBERG *holds the plates so that Ferguson can see them:* George . . . ?

FERGUSON: That shadow there! The right apex.

LEVINE: Yes—I was afraid of. . . .

HOCHBERG: Now, don't be an alarmist! *Sees something.* Mm! *Squints at the plate, and asks, gravely:* Have you examined the sputum? *Pause.*

LEVINE: I brought a specimen. *He takes out a bottle, wrapped in paper, and explains apologetically:* My microscope is broken.

HOCHBERG: We'll look at it here!

FERGUSON: Certainly! *He takes the bottle.* I'll have the path lab [2] check up on this. Is it anything important?

LEVINE: My wife.

---

[1] X-ray: discovered by Wilhelm Konrad Röntgen (1845-1922). It has since become so important an accessory that today a good physician would not set a broken finger without it.

[2] Path lab: hospital jargon for pathology laboratory.

FERGUSON: Oh.

HOCHBERG: Er . . . Dr. Ferguson, Dr. Levine! *They shake hands and exchange greetings.*

FERGUSON: I'll tend to this at once, Doctor.

LEVINE: Thanks. Do you think if I came back this evening——?

FERGUSON: Oh, yes, the report will be ready then. Drop into my room—106.

LEVINE: 106? *He turns to Hochberg. With nostalgia:* My old room.

FERGUSON: You interned here? Are you the—— Oh, of course. Bellevue, aren't you?

LEVINE *nods:* '23!

FERGUSON: Professor Dury mentions you quite often.

LEVINE: Dury? *To Hochberg:* He still remembers me. . . .

FERGUSON: He thinks a great deal of you.

HOCHBERG: George, here, is one of his prize pupils, too.

LEVINE: And does he want you to study abroad?

FERGUSON: Yes. I planned to go with Sauerbruch, but he has been forced to leave Germany.[1] So, instead

---

[1] "In the physician's professional relations, though divided by national lines, there remains the feeling that he belongs to a Guild that owes no local allegiance, which has neither king nor country, but whose work is in the world".—Sir William Osler, in "Counsels and Ideals".

Attempting to make the physician deny this, his fundamental creed, Hitler's Reich has merely succeeded in halting the progress of modern German medicine. Nazi intolerance forced not only all the prominent Jewish figures in medicine, but also non-Jews like Ernst Ferdinand Sauerbruch, greatest living German surgeon, to close their clinics and leave Germany in of that, I'm going to study under von Eiselsberg [1] in Vienna.

HOCHBERG: Hm! I remember when I was a student in Berlin, one of my classmates came to an examination in military uniform . . . sabre and all. Virchow looked at him, and said, "You! What are you doing here in that monkey suit? Your business is with death! Ours is with life!" Virchow was a man of science. He knew. [2] *He shakes his head.* I wonder what he would say to our beloved Germany today.

LEVINE: Yes. . . .

FERGUSON *to Hochberg:* Well, Laura prefers Vienna, anyway, so. . . . *To Levine:* I'm going on my honeymoon too, you see.

LEVINE: You'll find it difficult mixing the two. I know von Eiselsberg.

HOCHBERG: It's going to be very difficult. You don't know Laura.

despair. Not satisfied with expatriating their finest surgeons, the Nazis, with peculiar compassion, enforced anti-vivisection laws restricting their young surgeons from practicing . . . except on human subjects! Surgery, which is a fine art requiring, in addition to other things, the digital sensitivity of a pianist, demands incessant practice. Germany will see no more Sauerbruchs till she learns to respect the autonomy, the humanity, and the tolerance which are the spirit of medicine, and without it cannot exist.

[1] Anton von Eiselsberg: the foremost living Viennese surgeon.

[2] Rudolf Virchow, pathologist and anthropologist (1821-1902) made many important contributions to modern medicine.

Though I have taken some liberties in the telling, this anecdote has its basis in fact and was recounted to me with relish by an old pupil of the great Virchow.

FERGUSON: After a year in Vienna I'm working with Dr. Hochberg. So the real labor won't begin till I come back from Europe.

HOCHBERG: Oh, I'll drive you, George! With a whip, eh?

LEVINE: Lucky! *Retrospectively.* Yes. . . . I once looked forward to all that. *He sighs.*

HOCHBERG: Well, come, Levine. We'll go down to X-ray and read these pictures properly.

FERGUSON *holds up bottle:* And don't worry about this.

LEVINE: Thank you . . . thank you. *Exit Hochberg. Levine turns to Ferguson:* Remember, there's only one Hochberg. Every minute with him is precious.

FERGUSON: I won't miss a second of it.

Levine goes. Ferguson crosses to a long table at which Michaelson and Shorty are seated.

MICHAELSON (*who has been watching Levine and Ferguson*): He's telling *you,* huh?

FERGUSON *nods, smiles and looks for a particular book in the shelves:* Say, there's a damned interesting article on Hochberg in this week's A.M.A.[1]

FERGUSON: I know. *He finds the magazine and hands it over to Shorty, a small, chubby, good-natured, irrespon-*

---

[1] A.M.A.: the journal of the American Medical Association. The most widely read medical publication in the United States; published with the purpose of welding the medical profession into an efficient, competent body to guard against quackery and to preserve the highest standards of ethics and education.

sible, wise-cracking fellow, who takes life in his stride.
Here it is. You want to read this, Shorty.

Shorty sits down to read it.

MICHAELSON: Yep. I wish I could get in with him for
a year. . . .

FERGUSON *to Shorty:* What do you think of that first
case? The way he handled it? Beautiful job, isn't it?
Beautiful!

PETE, *interne, a tall, gawky lad, slow moving and casual
about everything but food, enters, fixing his stethoscope.
He drawls:* Say, George. . . .

SHORTY: Pete! Sweetheart! You're just the man I've
been looking for.

PETE *drily:* The answer is no.

SHORTY: Will you lend me your white tux vest for tonight? I've got. . . .

PETE *abruptly:* The answer is still no. *He turns to Ferguson.* That little——

SHORTY *sits down again:* Thanks!

PETE: You're welcome. *To Ferguson again:* The little
girl we just operated on is coming out of her ether nicely.
I was kind of worried about that preop [1] Insulin.[2]

FERGUSON: Why? How much did you give her?

PETE: Forty units.

---

[1] Preop: hospital jargon meaning "before operation".
[2] Insulin: an extract from the pancreas used in the treatment of diabetes.
The patient referred to has diabetes, and hence special preoperative treatment is required.

FERGUSON: Twenty would have been enough.

PETE: I know.

FERGUSON: Then why the hell did you give her forty? You might have hurt the kid.

PETE: Dr. Cunningham ordered it.

SHORTY: That dope—Cunningham!

FERGUSON: You should have told me before you gave it to her. I'm not going to have any patients go into shock on the operating table![1] Understand?

PETE: O.K.

FERGUSON *good-naturedly, slapping Pete on the head with a pamphlet:* If this happens again, Pete, you get your behind kicked in . . . and not by Cunningham!

PETE: O.K.

A Nurse, passing by, carrying a tray of medication, halts in the doorway, looks in and calls:

NURSE: Oh, Doctor Ferguson, that drink worked wonders. Bed three is sitting up and taking notice.

FERGUSON *laughs:* A new school of therapy!

SHORTY: Say, Jamison, you're not looking so hot. You ought to stay home one night and get some sleep.

JAMISON: Oh, I'm doing all right. *She laughs and goes.*

SHORTY: Yeah? I'll bet you are.

The loud speaker starts calling, "Dr. Bradley! Dr. Bradley!"

---

[1] Insulin shock: In diabetes, insulin is used to enable the body to utilize the abnormal amounts of sugar in the blood. Too much insulin, however, will reduce the sugar content of the blood below normal and throw the patient into a condition of shock.

PETE: Say, I'm hungry! Somebody got something to eat?

SHORTY: What, again? *Pete looks at him with scorn:* Lend me your white vest for tonight, will you, Pete? I'll fix up a date for you with that red-head.

Phone rings.

PETE *nodding at Ferguson:* Fix him up.

Ferguson laughs.

SHORTY: It'd do him good. That's the trouble with love —it kills your sex-life. . . . *Indicates the phone.* Pete! Phone!

PETE: I was once in love myself. *He starts for phone.* But when it began to interfere with my appetite. . . . Hell! No woman's worth that!

They laugh.

FERGUSON: Thing I like about you, Pete, is your romantic nature.

PETE *on phone:* Dr. Bradley! O.K. I'll be right up! *He hangs up.* Yep. At heart I'm just a dreamer.

SHORTY: At heart you're just a stinker!

PETE: Thanks!

SHORTY *quickly:* You're welcome!

Pete goes toward the door.

FERGUSON: Going upstairs, Pete?

PETE: Yep.

FERGUSON *gives him the bottle of sputum:* Will you take this to the path lab? Ask Finn to examine it and draw up a report.

PETE: O.K.

Enter Dr. Gordon.

FERGUSON: Tell him to give it special attention! It's a friend of Hochberg's.

SHORTY *follows Pete to door:* I take back what I said, Pete. You're a great guy, and I like you. Now, if you'll only lend me that white vest. . . .

PETE: No!

SHORTY: Stinker! *They exit.*

Gordon comes over to Ferguson.

GORDON (*his face grave*): Well . . . I just saw 401. He's a mighty sick boy. He may need another transfusion.

FERGUSON: We'll have to go pretty deep to find a good vein.

GORDON: That's what I'm worried about. If it comes up tonight I want you to be here to do it.

FERGUSON: Tonight?

GORDON: There are three donors on call.

FERGUSON: This is my night out. . . . My fiancée has made arrangements. . . . So I'm afraid I won't be here.

GORDON: I'm sorry, Ferguson. When the House needs you. . . .

FERGUSON: I'd like to, Doctor, but the same thing happened last week. I can't disappoint my fiancée again . . . or . . . *he smiles* . . . I won't have any.

MICHAELSON: Er—Dr. Gordon, couldn't I do that transfusion?

GORDON: I'm afraid not—the superficial veins are all

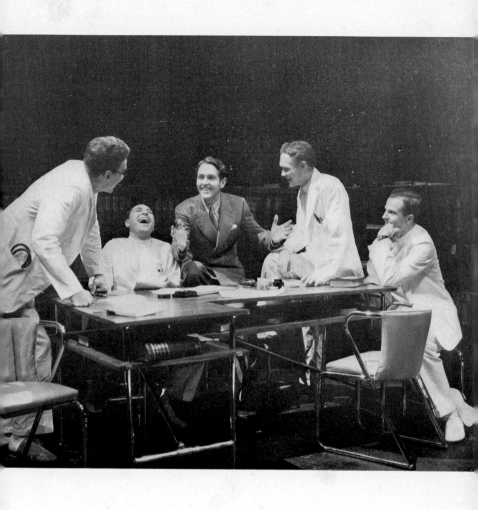

thrombosed.[1] Ferguson has followed the case from the start; he knows the veins we've used.

FERGUSON: Laidlaw knows the veins. . . .

GORDON: Frankly, I don't trust any of the other men on this case. I know I'm imposing, but I want this boy to have every possible chance. . . . *Pause.* He's a sick boy, Ferguson. What do you say?

FERGUSON: All right! I'll stay.

GORDON: Thanks! *He starts to go—turns back.* And if your sweetheart kicks up a fuss send her around to me. I'll tell her about my wife. Up at four-thirty this morning to answer the phone. Somebody had a bellyache. . . . *He laughs, nods and goes. Ferguson remains, dejected.*

FERGUSON: Damn it! I wanted to be with Laura, to-night.

MICHAELSON: That's tough, George. I'm sorry I couldn't help you out.

The loud speaker starts calling: "Dr. Manning! Dr. Manning!"

FERGUSON *rises and walks about:* Laura's going to be hurt. You'd think they'd have a little. . . .

NURSE *comes quickly down the corridor, looks in, and calls, a bit breathless:* Dr. Ferguson? *She sees him.* Dr. Ferguson, a woman just came in on emergency with a lacerated throat. She's bleeding terribly! Dr. Crane told me to tell you he can't stop it.

---

[1] Thrombosed vein: a plugged or occluded vein.

FERGUSON: Get her up to the operating-room. *He snaps his fingers.* Stat.[1] *She hurries off. He turns to Mac.* Drop that Mac, and order the O.R.! Come on! *Mac goes to a phone. To Michaelson:* Call an anaesthetist, will you? And locate Dr. Hochberg! Try the X-ray room!

MICHAELSON: Right! *He jumps to a phone. Exit Ferguson.*

MAC: Operating-room! . . . Emergency B! . . . Quick! . . . O.R.? . . . Set up the O.R. right away! Lacerated throat! Dr. Ferguson! Yes!

MICHAELSON: Find Dr. Hochberg! Right away! Emergency! . . . (*The loud speaker, which has been calling,* "Dr. Manning!" *changes to a louder and more persistent,* "Dr. Hochberg! Dr. Hochberg, Dr. Hochberg!") Well, try the X-ray room! . . . And locate the staff anaesthetist!

On phones, simultaneously.

In the back corridor we catch a glimpse of an orderly hurriedly pushing a rolling-stretcher on which the emergency patient is lying, crying hysterically. An interne on one side, and the nurse at the other are holding pads to her throat and trying to calm her.

FADE OUT

[1] Stat: hospital jargon for immediately.

Scene 2

THE *largest and the most expensive private room in the hospital. It is luxuriously furnished in the best of taste and tries hard to drive all clinical atmosphere out into the corridor. What the room can't eliminate, it attempts to disguise; not, however, with complete success. For there, behind a large, flowered screen, the foot of a hospital "gatch" bed peeps out, and in the corner we see a table with bottles of medication on it.*

Mr. Hudson, a large man, haunched, paunched and jowled, clad in pajamas and a lounging robe, is sitting up on a divan being shaved by the hospital barber.[1] He is talking to one of his business associates, a Mr. Mooney, who is a smaller, nattier, less impressive, and, at the moment, highly nervous edition of Hudson.

HUDSON *through a face full of lather:* We'll get that property, Mooney! And we'll get it now . . . on our own terms.

[1] The barber of mediaeval days is the great-granddaddy of the modern surgeon. He let blood, cupped, leeched, gave enemas, extracted teeth and treated wounds.

This particular barber would be delighted to learn the honorable antecedence of his profession, for, with the help of his white jacket, he tries, like many of his brethren, to resemble an interne, and is delighted when occasionally some near-sighted visitor does call him "Doctor".

MOONEY *marching impatiently to and fro:* How are you going to break that Clinton Street boom?

HUDSON: You get in touch with the real estate editor of every paper in town. Tell them we've decided to change the location of Hudson City from Clinton to . . . say Third Street. Map out a territory! Make it convincing!

A nurse enters with a bowl of flowers, places it on a small table, arranges the flowers, and departs.

MOONEY *hesitantly:* Think they'll believe it?

HUDSON: Sure. . . . Got a cigar?

MOONEY *produces one, then hesitates:* You're not supposed to smoke, you know.

HUDSON: I'm all right! Can't think without a cigar! *He takes it. The barber gives him a light. He puffs once or twice with huge relish.* Start negotiations with every realty owner in the new territory. Buy options! They'll believe that!

The barber finishes, starts to powder Hudson's face, but is waved away.

MOONEY: Oh yes. . . .

HUDSON: In the meantime sell ten of our houses on Clinton Street—including corners. Sell low!

MOONEY: Hey! We want that stuff!

HUDSON: Get Henderson! Form two dummy corporations—and sell to them.

MOONEY: Oh! . . . Yes, I think it'll work . . . that ought to bring down those prices.

The barber packs his shaving kit, and exits.

HUDSON: We'll wait till they're ready to take nickels . . . then our dummy corporations can grab all that property. . . . Mooney, we'll be excavating this Spring, yet.

Enter Dr. Hochberg. He sees Hudson smoking, frowns, goes to him, takes the cigar out of his mouth, and throws it away.

HOCHBERG: Didn't Doctor Whitman say no more cigars?

HUDSON *startled, his first impulse one of extreme annoyance:* Hochberg, please. . . . *He controls himself, turns to Mooney.*

MOONEY *glances at Hochberg, picks up his coat and hat:* Well, I'll be going now.

HUDSON *helps him into his coat:* Phone me!

MOONEY: I will. . . . Don't worry! *Shakes Hudson's hand.* Take care of yourself! *To Hochberg:* Goodbye, Doctor! *Hochberg nods. Exit Mooney.*

Hochberg watches Mooney go, then turns to Hudson and shakes his head.

HUDSON: Whitman's sending me home Tuesday, isn't he? What do you want to do? Make an invalid of me? *He goes to the phone.* Operator! Get me Vanderbilt 2-34—— *He gasps, an expression of pain crosses his face, his free hand goes to his breast.*

HOCHBERG *nods grimly:* Uh, huh! *Hudson glances at Hochberg guiltily, controls himself, continues on the phone.*

HUDSON: 3471!

HOCHBERG *goes to him, takes the phone out of his hand,*

puts it down, with an abrupt nod of the head toward the bed: You better lie down!

HUDSON: It's nothing. Just a. . . .

HOCHBERG *softly:* I know. Get into bed.

Hudson shakes his head and smiles to himself at Hochberg's persistence. Then he goes to the bed and lies down. Hochberg feels his pulse.

HUDSON: I tell you, I'm all right!

HOCHBERG: I don't understand people like you, John. Whitman is the best cardiac man in the country, but he can't give you a new heart! Don't you know that? Are you such a fool?

Enter Laura, a spirited, chic young lady; lithe, fresh, quick, modern, a trifle spoiled perhaps, but withal eminently warm, lovable and human.

LAURA: What's he done now, Hocky?

HUDSON: Hello, honey!

HOCHBERG: Laura!

LAURA *kissing Hudson:* How's my dad, today?

HUDSON: I'm fine, dear, just fine.

LAURA *takes Hochberg's hand:* And Hocky, wie gehts?

HOCHBERG: Laura, my dear, can't you do anything with him?

LAURA: Why? . . . Smoking again?

HOCHBERG: Yes.

LAURA: Oh, Dad!

HUDSON: Now, don't you start, Laura!

LAURA: But it's so foolish.

HUDSON: I have an important deal on, honey. Besides I'm all right. Whitman's sending me home Tuesday.

LAURA: I know, dear, and that's great! But it isn't going to do any good if you act this way. Can't you forget the office? Close it up! I mean that.

HOCHBERG: She's right, John—absolutely.

LAURA: What good is your money, damn it! if you can't enjoy it?

HUDSON: Well, it can still buy my little girl a honeymoon.

LAURA: I could spend my honeymoon right here! And have a swell time. As long as it's with George. . . . *To Hochberg:* Where is that man?

HOCHBERG: Upstairs—busy!

LAURA: Oh! *To her father:* So, are you going to behave yourself, Dad?

HUDSON *smiles and pinches her cheek:* Don't worry about me! I'm all right. . . . I'll live. *Deliberately changing the subject:* How was Doris' party last night?

LAURA: Noisy.

HUDSON: Not much fun, eh?

LAURA: Not much.

HUDSON: Too bad George couldn't be there.

LAURA: I spent most of the time upstairs with Doris' baby. It woke and wanted some attention. Babies are awfully human that way, aren't they? Do you know that Doris was going to let him cry himself to sleep? Can you imagine? ! . . . Believe me, when I have my baby, it's going to get all the care and love and attention it can use.

DR. HOCHBERG *chuckles:* You have the right instincts, Laura.

LAURA: Have I? *Rises.* I haven't had a real kiss in days. . . . Can I get George on the phone, Hocky?

HOCHBERG: He'll be down soon.

LAURA *goes to phone:* I want to see that man! *She picks up the phone.*

HOCHBERG *brusquely:* Better wait! *Laura looks at him, a bit resentfully.* He's in the operating room.

LAURA: Oh!

HUDSON: Er . . . while you're there, Laura, will you call the office like a good girl, and ask Henderson if. . . .

LAURA: No! *She hangs up sharply.*

HUDSON: But this is on my mind.

HOCHBERG: Again? John, you're a madman!

LAURA *quickly, with a tinge of bitterness:* And he's not the only one, Doctor Hochberg.

HUDSON *looks up at her quizzically, sees what's eating her, then turns to Hochberg:* God, they make a slave of that boy. And he doesn't get a dime! I can't see it.

HOCHBERG *smiles at that one:* He's not here for the money! He's here to learn. The harder he works the more he learns. If he wanted to make money he wouldn't have chosen medicine in the first place. You know, when he comes with me, his pay is only going to be $20 a week, but there's a chance to work. The man who's there with me now works from 16 to 18 hours a day. He even has a cot rigged up in one of the laboratories, where he sleeps sometimes.[1]

HUDSON: For $20 a week?

HOCHBERG *nods vigorously:* Yes, yes. . . . *He turns to Laura:* George is a fine boy with great promise. The next five years are crucial years in that boy's life. They're going to tell whether he becomes an important man or not.[2]

LAURA: George is an important man right now, Hocky, to me.

HOCHBERG: To *you.* . . .

LAURA: Well . . . I don't count?

HOCHBERG: Of course you do, dear!

LAURA *controls herself, turns to her father, abruptly changing the conversation:* What time shall I call for you Tuesday?

HUDSON *to Hochberg:* When can I get out of here?

HOCHBERG: In the morning. Eight—nine o'clock.

HUDSON: Good! *To Laura:* Have Martha prepare a big juicy steak—they've been starving me here.

HOCHBERG: No big steaks!

Hudson groans.

---

[1] Following the eminent example of Sir William Osler.

[2] "The education of most people ends upon graduation; that of the physician means a lifetime of incessant study".—Marx in Garrison's "History of Medicine".

How much truer this is, then, for a man in medicine who wishes to extend himself in special fields above and beyond those normally trodden by his colleagues!

Ferguson enters, tired and upset.

LAURA: George! *She goes to him.*

FERGUSON: Hello, darling! *He kisses her.*

LAURA: Why so glum, dear—toothache?

FERGUSON *grins—looks at her hat:* Where did you get that hat?

LAURA: Don't you like it?

FERGUSON: Looks like a sailboat! *Laura wrinkles her face, pretending to be on the verge of tears.* No, it's becoming! You look beautiful . . . doesn't she, Doctor Hochberg?

HOCHBERG *disparagingly:* Hm—she looks all right.

LAURA *laughs:* I'll kill that man.

HOCHBERG: You should have seen the brat when I delivered her. *The recollection is too much for him. He looks at Laura, shakes his head, and chuckles.*

FERGUSON *goes to the bedside:* And Dad—I guess we're going to lose our best patient Tuesday.

LAURA: Isn't it marvelous?

FERGUSON: Did you ever see him look so healthy?

HUDSON: I feel fine, George! Good enough to eat a big steak!

HOCHBERG *grunts:* Mm!

HUDSON: Oh, by the way, George, my secretary's tending to the wedding invitations. Better get your list in to him. And see him about your visas, too. He'll tend to all that.

FERGUSON *to Laura:* You know—I still can't believe it's going to happen! I mean just happen!

LAURA: Neither can I.

FERGUSON: Vienna's going to be lots of fun.

LAURA: Fun? You don't know. Wait till you've seen the Prater. It's Coney Island with a lift! Lights all over . . . and those lovely people all laughing and happy . . . and the whole place just tinkling with music.

FERGUSON: I've always had a yen to hear Strauss on his home grounds.

HOCHBERG *softly:* When I visited Von Eiselsberg his students spent all their time working—with an occasional glass of beer for relaxation. That's what George's Vienna is going to be, Laura.

George and Laura are brought up sharp. Enter a nurse with a wheel-chair.

NURSE: Time for your sun bath, sir.

HUDSON: Oh—go away!

HOCHBERG: Come on, Mr. Hudson, no nonsense.

HUDSON: Aw, hell, I can walk, I'm no cripple!

LAURA: Sit down, dad.

HUDSON *sits in the chair. The nurse tucks a blanket around him. Hudson grumbles to himself:* Treat me like a God damned baby! . . . *To nurse:* Get me that report, will you?

HOCHBERG: John. . . .

HUDSON: I can read, can't I? There's nothing the matter with my eyes. . . . For God's sake. . . . *He turns to George and Laura:* Don't you listen to that old fogey! You kids enjoy yourselves. You're only young once.

The nurse wheels him out. Hochberg watches him go and nods.

HOCHBERG: Yes, that's true enough! *He looks at Ferguson and Laura, a twinkle in his eyes, and sits down as if he were there to stay.*

FERGUSON: You don't need me yet, Doctor Hochberg, do you?

HOCHBERG: Why not?

LAURA *threateningly:* Hocky!

HOCHBERG *rises, grinning like a little boy who's had his joke:* All right! *To Ferguson:* I'll call you when I want you. *He goes.*

LAURA *softly:* Sweetheart! *She holds out her hands to him.*

FERGUSON *taking them:* Darling! *He draws her up out of the chair to him.*

LAURA: How's my boy?

FERGUSON *stares at her in adoration. He almost whispers:* You're lovely. . . . Lovely, Laura.

Big hug.

LAURA: If you knew how I've been aching for this. *Silence for a moment, as she clings to him.* Three months! *She sighs deeply.* I don't know how I can live till then.

FERGUSON *tenderly:* Sweet! They're going to be long— those three months—terribly.

LAURA: Yes, I know—I hate to think of them! *She takes*

his hand, leads him to a huge easy-chair: Come here
and——

FERGUSON: Ah!

LAURA: Sit down! *She pushes him down into the chair
and curls up on his lap. Then she takes his head in her
hands and scrutinizes his face.* Let me look at you. *She
shakes her head.* You're getting thin, young man! And
your eyes are tired.

FERGUSON: I didn't have much sleep last night. It was
a pretty sick house.

LAURA: You're overworked. . . . *Pulls his head over on
her shoulder.* And I don't like it one bit. *Pause.* You
know, you've spoiled everything for me. *Ferguson raises
his head, Laura pushes his head back.* I was thinking
last night, all the music and noise and fun . . . didn't
mean a thing without you. I don't seem to get a kick out
of life any more, unless you're around. *She pauses.* And
that's not very often, is it?

FERGUSON: Darling, we'll make up for it all . . . later
on. Honestly.

LAURA: I don't know if we can, George. Last night,
for instance. If you had been there—perfect! Now's it's—
gone. You see, dearest, the way I feel, if I had you every
minute from now on, it wouldn't be enough. *Ferguson
starts to speak, she puts her hands over his lips.* I wish I'd
lived all my life with you. I wish I'd been born in the
same room with you, and played in the same streets.

FERGUSON *smiles:* I'm glad you missed them. They were

ordinary and gloomy. They might have touched you . . . changed you. . . . *He cups her face in his hands and looks at her.* About seven months ago there was a boy here who'd been blind from birth. We operated on him—successfully. One night I showed him the stars—for the first time. He looked at them a moment and began to cry like a baby, because, he said, they were so lovely, and—he might never have seen them. When I look at you, Laura, I get something of that feeling. I . . . I can't tell you how large a part of me you've become, Laura! You're. . . .

The loud speaker is heard calling: "Dr. Ferguson! Dr. Ferguson. . . ."

Oh, damn it! . . .

LAURA: Don't move! *She clutches him tightly.*

FERGUSON: It's no use, Laura! That's my call! Let me up!

LAURA: No!

FERGUSON: Come on! *He rises, lifting her in his arms, kisses her, sets her on her feet.*

LAURA: Oh! You spoiled it.

He goes to the phone, picks up the receiver. Laura finds her vanity case . . . powder and lipstick.

FERGUSON: Dr. Ferguson! . . . Yes! . . . Oh! Yes, sir! . . . Yes, doctor! I'll be ready. . . . I'll tend to all that. Right! *He hangs up—turns to Laura.*

LAURA: All right, go on—go to work!

FERGUSON: I won't be needed for half an hour yet.

LAURA: Well, I have to go to my hairdresser's and make myself beautiful for tonight.

FERGUSON: Laura, dear, I. . . .

LAURA: And what a night we're to going to have! Doris asked us over there, but I want you to myself. I want to go to that cute little road house where the food and the music were so good—then a long drive up the Hudson—and, darling, there's a full moon, tonight!

FERGUSON: Laura, I've some bad news. You won't be upset, will you?

LAURA: Why?

FERGUSON: I can't make it tonight. I have to stay in. . . .

LAURA *almost in tears:* Again?

FERGUSON: I'm so sorry, dear. I tried to duck out of it, but I couldn't. There's a transfusion I have to do.

LAURA: What time? I'll wait.

FERGUSON: Better not! It depends on the patient. I've just got to be around and ready!

LAURA: Are you the only one here who can do that transfusion?

FERGUSON: Dr. Gordon seems to think so!

LAURA: George! They're overworking you. It's not fair. . . .

FERGUSON: I don't mind it so much for myself . . . only. . . .

LAURA *dully:* No? Well I do. *Pause. Then Laura continues in a low voice, suddenly hoarse:* I was planning so much on tonight.

FERGUSON: Don't you think I was, Laura? All week I've been looking forward to it.

LAURA: Sure. I know.

FERGUSON: You're not sore?

LAURA: It's not your fault. I don't imagine it's much fun for you, either——

FERGUSON: Fun! If you knew how fed up I can be with this place sometimes. . . .

LAURA: George, I'm so low—I've been this way for weeks.

FERGUSON: Damn Gordon! Laidlaw could have done that transfusion.

LAURA: Oh, George, what's our life going to be like?

FERGUSON *gently:* Pretty grand, I should say.

LAURA: How can it be? How can it?

FERGUSON: Dear . . . we'll go out tomorrow instead. Mac promised to take my floor. And we'll have a swell time. Saturday's more fun anyway.

LAURA: It's not just tonight! It's all the nights.

FERGUSON: Darling! You're exaggerating! You're. . . .

LAURA: No, I'm not.

FERGUSON: What do you expect me to do? I want to get out . . . I want to enjoy myself . . . but I can't, that's all. I can't.

LAURA: George, I know this is important to you . . . and if it's going to help you . . . I can go on like this for another three months . . . for another year and three months; but when we come back to New York, let's arrange our lives like human beings. You can open up an office and have regular hours . . . specialize!

FERGUSON: If I work with Hochberg, darling, I won't have the time to go into practice.

LAURA: That's just it. I know Hocky. I'll never see you then, George.

FERGUSON: But, Laura. . . . *He laughs nervously.* I've plugged all my life just in the hope that some day I'd have a chance to work with a man like Hochberg. . . . Why. . . .

LAURA: I couldn't go on this way. I just couldn't. . . . I'd rather break off now, and try to forget you. . . .

FERGUSON: Laura! Don't ever say a thing like that!

LAURA: I mean it—it would kill me. But I'd rather die quickly than by slow torture. I can't. . . . *The loud speaker is calling him. Ferguson and Laura stand there both in anguish.* They're calling you.

FERGUSON: I know. *He hesitates a moment . . . goes to the phone:* Dr. Ferguson! Yes . . . who? South 218 . . . yes? . . . well, call Dr. Cunningham. It's his case . . . let him. *Suddenly his voice becomes brittle.* When? What's her temperature? . . . Pulse? . . . Is she pale? . . . Perspiring? . . . Did she ask for food before she became unconscious? . . . No! No more insulin! Absolutely. I'll be right down. *He hangs up.* I have to go now, Laura. And please—please don't worry. *He bends down to kiss her. She turns her face away. He straightens up and regards her with a worried expression.*

FERGUSON: As bad as that?

LAURA *in a low voice—a bit husky with emotion:* Yes.

FERGUSON *forcing a smile:* Things will straighten themselves out.

LAURA: No, they won't.

Pause. Ferguson pulls himself together, looks towards the door.

FERGUSON: I'll see you tomorrow night dear? Right?

LAURA: Yes. *She puts on her hat.* Think it over, George! We'll have to come to some decision!

FERGUSON: Oh Laura, will you please. . . .

LAURA: I mean it! Absolutely!

FERGUSON *pauses for a moment in the doorway:* All right . . . all right!

Ferguson goes. Laura stands there a moment, the picture of frustration and woe, then she walks in a little circle, crying quietly.

BLACK OUT

Scene 3

A BED, *screened off from the others, in a corner of the children's ward. The entire wall, separating ward from corridor, is framed in glass panels, so that the nurse on duty out there can always keep a watchful eye over the youngsters.*

A little girl of ten is lying back, eyes closed, skin pale and clammy. Her father stands at the foot of the bed, gazing fearfully at his little daughter. He is wan and unkempt, his hair disheveled, his eyes sunken, his collar open, tie awry—the picture of despair. His wife is standing beside the child, weeping.

At the phone is a young student-nurse, Barbara Dennin. She is speaking rapidly into the phone.

NURSE: South 218! . . . Calling Dr. Ferguson! At once!

MRS. SMITH: She's so pale, Barney. . . . She's so pale!

MR. SMITH: Where's Cunningham? . . . Why isn't he here? *To the nurse:* Miss Dennin! Can't you do something?

NURSE: Dr. Ferguson will be right here, sir!

Enter Dr. Cunningham, a dignified, impressive-looking gentleman, immaculately attired, goatee, pince-nez, throaty voice—just a bit too much of the "professional

*manner", arrived at in this instance by a certain false
philosophy which one occasionally finds in the profession.
Cunningham believes that nine patients out of ten will
be cured by nature anyway, and the tenth will die no
matter what the physician does for him. This system of
logic concludes that impressing the patient and assuaging
his fears are more important than keeping up with medical journals and the march of treatment. The sad part
of it is that Cunningham is a successful practitioner—
successful, that is, in terms of bank account. True, most
of his colleagues look down on him with scorn, but he has
a magnificent Park Avenue office, with all the impressive
equipment, wealthy patients, and political influence—
which, although he is not a member of the staff, has
gained him the "courtesy" of the hospital—meaning that
he may bring his patients here for hospitalization.*

NURSE: Dr. Cunningham! Thank God you're here!

MRS. SMITH: Dr. Cunningham! My baby! She's fainted!
She's. . . .

CUNNINGHAM: Now please . . . please, Mrs. Smith! *He
takes off his coat, turns to Barbara:* What's happened
here?

NURSE: Complete collapse . . . about two minutes
ago. . . .

CUNNINGHAM: Let's see the chart! *She hands him the
chart. He looks at it, frowns, shakes his head.* Hm! This
is bad! *He takes Dot's wrist and feels the pulse, closing
his eyes.*

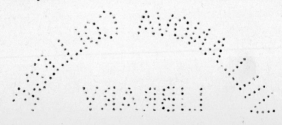

NURSE: Pulse is barely. . . .

CUNNINGHAM: Sh! Quiet, please! . . . *Silence.* Hm! . . . Let me have my stethoscope! *She takes his stethoscope out of his bag and hands it to him. He listens to Dot's heart. His frown deepens.* Diabetic coma!

MRS. SMITH: Doctor! . . . you've got to save her!

MR. SMITH: Rose . . . come here!

CUNNINGHAM: Miss Dennin—— *He indicates Mrs. Smith with a gesture of the head.*

NURSE *takes Mrs. Smith's arm:* You'll have to wait outside. . . . Just a moment. . . .

MRS. SMITH: Oh, my God!

Barbara leads them out, then returns.

CUNNINGHAM: Prepare some insulin! At once . . . forty units . . . with fifty grams of glucose.

BARBARA: But, sir, Dr. Ferguson advised against insulin. . . .

CUNNINGHAM: Ferguson? You please take your orders from me . . . forty units! Quick!

BARBARA: Yes, sir.

Ferguson enters the room. Dr. Cunningham glances at him, nods curtly, and turns to Barbara.

CUNNINGHAM: Please, hurry that!

FERGUSON *looks at the patient, shakes his head:* I was afraid of shock!

CUNNINGHAM: This isn't shock! It's diabetic coma!

FERGUSON, *his brow wrinkled, looks at the patient again:* Her temperature's subnormal?

CUNNINGHAM *impatiently:* Yes! *To Barbara:* Is that insulin ready yet?

FERGUSON: I beg your pardon, Doctor, but isn't insulin contra-indicated here?

CUNNINGHAM: No. It's our last chance.

Ferguson bites his lips to restrain himself. Cunningham takes the hypo from Barbara and presses out the air bubbles.

FERGUSON: Doctor, I mean no offense, but I've studied this case history, and it looks like shock . . . not coma!

CUNNINGHAM *pauses—looks at the patient, shakes his head:* No . . . no. . . .

FERGUSON: But, the clinical picture is so clear-cut. . . . Look at the patient! She's pale, cold, clammy, temperature subnormal. She's complained of hunger! Sudden onset!

CUNNINGHAM *angrily:* Suppose you let me handle this case, young man. *To Barbara:* Prepare that arm!

Barbara swabs the arm. Cunningham leans over the patient. Ferguson hesitates a moment, then goes to Cunningham, puts his hand on Cunningham's arm.

FERGUSON: Please, doctor! Call in one of the other men! . . . Ask them! Anybody!

CUNNINGHAM: There's no time! Take your hand off!

FERGUSON: That insulin's going to prove fatal.

CUNNINGHAM *wavers a moment, uncertain, hesitant, then he turns on Ferguson:* Get out of here, will you? I don't want any interruption while I'm treating my patient! *He shakes Ferguson's arm off. . . . Bends to admin-*

*ister the hypo, hesitates a moment, then straightens up
... confused and worried. Ferguson, with sudden resolve,
takes the hypo from Cunningham's fingers and squirts
out the insulin.* Here! What are you. . . . Why did you
do that, you fool?

FERGUSON *ignores him, turns to Barbara, his voice crisp
and cool:* Shock position! *Barbara goes to the foot of the
bed, turns the ratchet that elevates the foot of the bed.
Ferguson dashes to the door, looks out, calls down the
corridor:* Nurse! Nurse!

A NURSE *answers from down the corridor:* Yes, sir?

FERGUSON: Sterile glucose! Quick! And a thirty c.c.
syringe.

BARBARA: Some glucose here, sir, all ready!

FERGUSON: How much?

BARBARA: Fifty grams!

FERGUSON: Good! Half of that will do! Apply a tourni-
quet . . . right arm!

BARBARA: Yes, sir!

FERGUSON *calls down the corridor:* Never mind the glucose—a hypo of adrenalin!

The nurse's voice answers: Yes, sir.

FERGUSON *turns up the corridor:* Nurse, nurse! Some hot
packs . . . and blankets! Quick . . . come on . . . hurry!
*He starts to return to the patient, but Dr. Cunningham,
who has sufficiently recovered from his shock, blocks
Ferguson's path.*

CUNNINGHAM: What do you think you're doing? I'll

DOROTHY: Dr. George . . . my operation hurts me here. . . .

FERGUSON *sympathetically:* Oh! We'll fix that up in a minute! *To Cunningham:* An opium suppository, doctor?

CUNNINGHAM: No! *To Barbara:* Morphine! A twelfth!

BARBARA: Yes, sir. *She goes.*

CUNNINGHAM *turns his glance on Ferguson:* I ought to report you, of course! You're a damned, meddling young puppy. . . . *He hesitates a moment.* However . . . under the circumstances, I guess I can afford to be lenient . . . this time. But if you ever dare interfere again in any of my cases . . . !

Mr. and Mrs. Smith enter. They rush to the bedside.

MRS. SMITH *crying and laughing:* Dorothy, my darling.

MR. SMITH: Dots! Dots!

MRS. SMITH: Are you all right, my baby? *She kisses Dot.* My baby!

DOROTHY: Oh! . . . my operation, mother. . . .

CUNNINGHAM: Careful, Mrs. Smith. . . .

MR. SMITH: Careful, Rose!

MRS. SMITH: Yes . . . yes . . . of course. Did I hurt my darling?

CUNNINGHAM: Now, the child's been through quite an ordeal. You mustn't excite her. I want her to have some rest . . . you'd better. . . . *Indicating the door with his hand.*

MR. SMITH: Yes, come, Rose. . . . She's weak. . . . *To Dot:* Go to sleep, darling.

MRS. SMITH: Goodbye, dear! *She kisses her.* Is there anything mother can bring you, darling?

DOROTHY *sleepily*: No, mama. . . .

Mr. Smith kisses the child, takes his wife's arm and leads her away.

CUNNINGHAM *turns to Ferguson*: Order a blood sugar! If there are any new developments phone my secretary at once!

MRS. SMITH *to Cunningham*: She'll be all right, Doctor?

CUNNINGHAM: Yes . . . yes. . . . You call me tonight!

Dr. Cunningham, Mr. and Mrs. Smith start to go.

MRS. SMITH *as they exit, to Cunningham*: Doctor, how can I ever thank you enough for this?

FERGUSON *goes to Dorothy*: Well, young lady, how about getting some sleep?

DOROTHY: O.K. Dr. George!

FERGUSON: Close your eyes!

DOROTHY: But don't go away!

FERGUSON *sits on bedside*: No. . . . I'll sit right here! Come on! *Dorothy takes his hand, shuts her eyes, and dozes off. Enter Barbara with hypo. Ferguson whispers:* She won't need that!

BARBARA: Did Dr. Cunningham say anything to you?

FERGUSON: No. *He stares down at Dorothy:* Pretty kid, isn't she?

BARBARA: I was scared we were going to lose her.

FERGUSON *touches the sleeping child's hair, and murmurs:* She has hair like Laura's.

BARBARA: What, doctor?

FERGUSON: Nothing. . . . Nothing. . . .

BARBARA: I think it was wonderful of you to stand up against Dr. Cunningham that way! I. . . .

FERGUSON *annoyed, turns to hypo, etc., and says a bit curtly:* Better clean up that mess.

BARBARA: Yes, sir. *She puts hypos, etc., on trays. Suddenly her trembling fingers drop the hypo. It splinters with a crash.*

FERGUSON *angrily:* Here! *Glances over at the sleeping child.* What's the matter with you?

BARBARA: I'm sorry. I was just . . . nervous, I guess. . . .

FERGUSON *looks at her a moment. She is a soft, feminine girl.* . . . *Her jet black hair and serious, large brown eyes are set off to pretty advantage by the blue-and-white student-nurse uniform. She has a simple, naive quality that lends her an air of appealing wistfulness. He sees how genuinely nervous she is . . . and smiles to reassure her:* Has Cunningham been treating you too?

BARBARA *smiles:* No, sir. This is my first case with a sick child and I got to like her an awful lot. I guess that was. . . .

FERGUSON: I see. What's your name?

BARBARA: Barbara Dennin.

FERGUSON: You're going to be a swell nurse, Barbara!

BARBARA: Thanks!

FERGUSON: Now, take my advice! I know just how you feel—nerves all tied up in a knot . . . want to yell! Feel the same way myself. . . . You get as far away from here as you can, tonight. Have a good time! Relax! Forget hospital! Tomorrow you'll be all right.

BARBARA: I . . . I can't. I have an exam in Materia Medica tomorrow.

FERGUSON: Materia Medica? . . . Hm! . . . I think I have some notes that may help you. . . . I'll leave them with the orderly on the first floor, and you can get them on your way down.

BARBARA: Thanks.

FERGUSON: May help you a bit. You won't have to cram all night, anyway.

The loud speaker is calling "Dr. Ferguson." Mary, another and much older nurse, enters with a basin, etc.

MARY: Your call, Doctor Ferguson?

FERGUSON *listening:* Yes. Are you on duty here now?

MARY: Yes, sir.

FERGUSON: If she wakes with any pain, give her an opium suppository! If her temperature goes below normal, call me! I'll be in.

MARY: Tonight, too?

FERGUSON *almost savagely:* Yes, tonight, too! *His name is called louder, more insistent. He turns to the door, mutters to the loud speaker:* All right! All right! I'm coming! *He goes. Mary turns to stare after him, her eyebrows raised in surprise.*

MARY: Gee! Ain't he snappy today?

Barbara simply stares after him.

BLACK OUT

Scene 4

A TINY, sombre, austere, cell-like room, with hardly enough space for its simple furnishings—a cot-bed, a bureau, a desk, a chair, a small book-case and a wash-basin. On the bureau is a small radio—the one luxury in the room. On the walls are two framed diplomas—the sole decorations. The room is untidy—as all internes' rooms are; the bed is messed, it being customary for internes to use it as a lounge; the books are piled irregularly on the book-shelves, on the desk, on the bureau, and on the floor.

A moonlit night filters in through a single square window.

Ferguson, wearing spectacles, is at his desk, reading, by the light of a desk lamp, a ponderous medical tome. Occasionally he jots down a note.

A knock at the door.

FERGUSON *without looking up, in a tired voice:* Come in!

Enter Shorty in a stiff bosom shirt, collar, white vest.

SHORTY *triumphantly:* Well, I got the vest....

FERGUSON: That's good.

SHORTY: Can you lend me a tie, George? Mine is—er——

Ferguson rises and wearily goes to his dresser, finds a tux bow tie, hands it to Shorty.

FERGUSON: Here you are, Shorty. *He sits down again to his book.*

SHORTY: Thanks! Say, do you mind making a bow for me? I can never get these things straight.

FERGUSON: Come here! I'll try. *He starts to tie Shorty's bow.*

SHORTY: Drink in my room . . . if you want one.

FERGUSON: I don't think so, Shorty!

SHORTY: Good drink! . . . Ginger ale, sugar and alcohol . . . out of the large jar in the path lab. . . .

FERGUSON: Stand still, will you? *After fumbling nervously with the tie, he makes a bad job of it.* Oh, hell! I can't do it! Sorry! *He undoes the tie.* Ask Laidlaw!

SHORTY *looks askance at Ferguson:* Nerves, young fellow! . . . Better see a Doctor about that!

PETE *pokes in his head:* Anything to eat in here?

FERGUSON: Some chocolate!

PETE: Good! *Enters—comes up to desk.*

FERGUSON: Here! *Gives him a chunk. Shorty starts to go.* Have a good time, Shorty!

SHORTY *confidently:* I will.

PETE *stands there, eating chocolate:* Hope she gives in without a struggle.

SHORTY: No fun, you dope—without a struggle. *Exits.*

PETE: Oh yeah? *Calls after him.* Well, take off my vest before you start. I don't want any stains on it. *He returns to the desk and points to the chocolate.* Now can I have some of that myself! *He reaches over and breaks off a piece of chocolate.*

FERGUSON *smiles:* Who was the first piece for?

PETE: Oh that? That was for my tapeworm. *He holds up the chocolate.* This is for me. *Pops it into his mouth. Ferguson laughs a tired laugh, and hands him the rest of the large bar, anxious to get rid of him.*

FERGUSON: Here, take it all, Pete!

PETE: Thanks! What a lousy dinner we had tonight! Fish! . . . Oh, how I hate fish!

FERGUSON: Friday night.

PETE: Yeah! Say! What are *you* doing in?

FERGUSON: 341 may need a transfusion. . . .

PETE: A lot of good that'll do him! *Stuffs his mouth with chocolate.* For Christ's sake . . . he passed out. . . .

FERGUSON: No?

PETE: About ten minutes ago.

FERGUSON *slowly:* Gee, that's too bad!

PETE *jamming in a huge chunk of chocolate:* Yeah! Say, I'm hungry. . . . I'm going to run out to Fleischer's and grab a sandwich. Will you keep an eye on my floor till I get back?

FERGUSON: All right! Hurry it, will you? . . . I may be going out myself.

PETE: Be right back! *Exits.*

Ferguson sits there a moment, staring blankly at the wall. Finally he sighs, wearily closes the book, pushes it

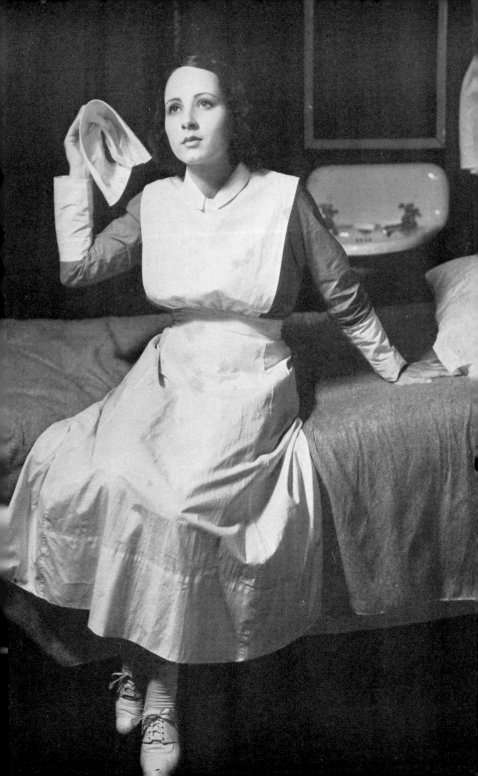

*away, takes off his spectacles, puts them in a case, and
reaches for the phone.*

FERGUSON: Outside wire, please! . . . Atwater 9-0032. . . .
Yes. . . . Hello! Hello! Is Miss Hudson there? Dr. Ferguson calling. . . . Yes. . . . Hello, Laura! . . . How are you
dear? . . . Feeling better? . . . Oh! . . . Well, look dear,
I can make it tonight, after all. What? . . . Oh, don't be
silly! . . . But darling . . . we'll work that out! We'll find
some. . . . It's so far away, yet. . . . Why talk about . . . ?
Listen Laura! That chance to work with Hochberg is
one of the best breaks I've ever had! You don't expect
me to throw it over, like that, at a moment's notice,
simply because you have some crazy idea that. . . . No,
no! I don't want to even talk about it, tonight. I'm tired,
Laura. It's been a hell of a day! Three operations and
. . . I can't think! I can't make an important decision
tonight . . . in a minute! Oh, Laura! What the hell are
you doing? Punishing me? . . . All right, Laura. *A knock
at the door.* All right. . . . I'll see you tomorrow night!
. . . Yes . . . yes . . . goodbye! *He hangs up, somewhat
sharply, then wearily goes to the door, opens it. Dr. Levine
is standing there.*

LEVINE: I'm sorry if I. . . .

FERGUSON: Oh, no! Come on in, Dr. Levine!

DR. LEVINE *murmurs a hardly audible thanks and enters. He looks about, touches the desk, smiles, nods, and
murmurs almost to himself:* Yes. . . . Yes . . . it certainly

is nice! Six years . . . like yesterday. *Looks at his watch:* Think that report is ready?

FERGUSON: I'll see. *Takes phone.*

LEVINE: Oh, don't trouble!

FERGUSON: That's. . . . *Into phone:* Hello! Path-lab, please! *To Dr. Levine:* What did Dr. Hochberg find?

LEVINE: He left it for the X-ray man to read.

FERGUSON *into phone:* Hello! . . . Dr. Finn? . . . Ferguson! What about that sputum? . . . Oh! *To Dr. Levine:* Under the microscope, now. *Into phone:* Fine! Hurry that through, will you? . . . And send it down to my room! . . . Yes. Thanks! *He hangs up.* A few minutes . . . I hope it's nothing. . . .

LEVINE *nods:* Poor Katherine! She's had so much. Things were so different when I was here . . . before I married.

FERGUSON: Yes . . . Professor Dury told me.

LEVINE: Dury? I know just what he says: Levine—the fool!—wealthy mother—chance to work with Hochberg —to be somebody. Threw it all away . . . for a pretty face. *He laughs to himself, sadly*—Hm . . . Dury!

FERGUSON: Your mother? Hasn't she . . . ? *Dr. Levine shakes his head.* Not yet? . . . Well, she'll come around to your way.

LEVINE *shakes his head again:* No. When I married Katherine, a gentile, and my mother disowned me . . . it must have broken her heart. But still, she was doing the right thing from her point of view. . . . *He sighs.* Poor

Katherine! I didn't count on that! East side! Tenements! Fifty-cent patients! Poverty! Dirt! Struggle! *He shakes his head*. I don't know. Maybe it would have been better for her the other way . . . maybe. *He smiles sadly at Ferguson*. Burnt offerings! Jehovah and Aesculapius![1] They both demand their human sacrifice. . . . *Pauses*. Medicine! Why do we kill ourselves for it?

FERGUSON: I don't know. I often wonder, myself, whether it was worth the grind of working my way through college and med school. . . .

LEVINE: Med school, too?

FERGUSON: Yes.

LEVINE: I don't see how you kept up with classes.

FERGUSON: I managed.

LEVINE: Terrific grind!

FERGUSON: It wasn't much fun . . . but, still . . . I guess it's the only thing I really want to do. . . . *Pause*. My dad used to say, "Above all is humanity!" He was a fine man —my dad. A small town physician—upstate. When I was about thirteen, he came to my room one night and apologized because he was going to die. His heart had gone bad on him. He knew if he gave up medicine and took it easy he could live for twenty years. But he wanted to go right on, wanted to die in harness. . . . And he did. *Pause*. Above all else is humanity—that's a big thought. So big that alongside of it you and I don't

---

[1] Aesculapius: Greek God of Medicine.

really matter very much. That's why we do it, I guess.

LEVINE: You're right of course! Ah . . . it's not good—too much suffering! Kills things in you. . . . A doctor shouldn't have to worry about money! That's one disease he's not trained to fight. It either corrupts him . . . or it destroys him. *He sighs.* Well . . . maybe some day the State will take over Medicine. . . .

FERGUSON: Before we let the State control medicine, we'd have to put every politician on the operating table, and cut out his acquisitive instincts.

LEVINE *laughs:* That, I'm afraid, would be a major operation!

FERGUSON *smiles:* Yes. . . . *Then he becomes serious again, working himself up, thinking of Laura.* But, it *is* a danger! We can't allow outside forces, or things . . . or people to interfere with us. . . . We can't! And, if they do, we've got to bar them out . . . even if we have to tear out our hearts to do it. . . . *Levine looks puzzled. He can't quite follow this. Ferguson suddenly realizes the personal turn his thoughts have taken, sees Levine's bewilderment, and stops short. He laughs, a bit self-conscious.* I'm sorry. I guess that's a bit off the track . . . just something personal.

LEVINE *smiles:* Oh! Yes. . . .

A knock at the door. Ferguson goes to the door. An orderly is there.

ORDERLY: Dr. Ferguson?

FERGUSON: Yes?

ORDERLY: Dr. Finn sent this down! *He hands Ferguson a printed report.*

FERGUSON: Oh, yes, thanks! *Orderly goes. Ferguson is about to hand it to Levine.* Doctor. . . . *Ferguson glances at it and suddenly stiffens.* One second!

LEVINE *suddenly becomes tense, too:* Dr. Ferguson! Is that. . . . ?

FERGUSON *in a strained, brittle voice:* Wait! *He goes to the phone:* Path Lab!

LEVINE: Is that for me?

Ferguson doesn't answer him.

FERGUSON: Path Lab? . . . Dr. Finn? . . . Ferguson! That report you just sent me . . . are you positive? . . . Make sure! Look again. . . .

LEVINE: Is that the finding on my? . . .

FERGUSON *over the phone:* Yes . . . Yes. . . . Clear as that? *Slowly.* I'm afraid you're right. *He hangs up slowly, turns to Levine, hands him the card in silence.*

LEVINE *takes it, reads it. He droops. His fingers tremble, the card falls to the ground. After a moment's silence he wets his lips and murmurs, almost inaudibly:* I knew it . . . I knew it. . . .

FERGUSON: Gee, I wish I could tell you how sorry I. . . .

LEVINE: Tuberculosis! Oh, my poor Katherine! *He sits down on the bed and stares vacantly ahead.* What are we going to do, now?

FERGUSON *goes to the bed, sits down next to him, tenderly puts a hand on his shoulder:* She'll come through, all right! You'll see. *A silence. Dr. Levine pulls himself together.* Perhaps if you took her to a drier climate. . . .

LEVINE: Maybe . . . maybe! *He rises.* That means . . . giving up the little practice I have . . . means starting all over again. I don't know if we can do it. We're not young, any longer. I don't know. . . .

Dr. Levine turns toward the door.

FERGUSON: Is there anything I can do?

LEVINE: No, thanks! Thanks! *Exit Dr. Levine.*

Ferguson stands there a moment, staring after him. Enter Pete.

PETE *sucking his teeth with great gusto:* Boy, what a roast-beef sandwich I had! Mm! *He sucks his teeth louder.* Have you got a . . . oh, yeah! *He reaches over, and takes a tongue-depresser out of Ferguson's breast pocket. Pete splits the depresser, and using one of the splinters as a tooth-pick, continues to make even a greater noise with his lips. Ferguson, pretty near the cracking point, turns his back on Pete. Pete goes to the radio, and tunes in on a loud jazz number. He flops down onto the bed—sucks his teeth.* Going out?

FERGUSON: No!

PETE: Change your mind?

FERGUSON: Yes.

PETE: Boy, you know that Miss Simpson down in the X-ray lab—— She was over at Fleischer's. Next table to mine. Say—she's swell all dressed up in street clothes. I looked at her for ten minutes without recognizing her. I guess maybe it was because I wasn't looking at her face. *Sucks his teeth.* Luscious! She had one of those tight black silk dresses . . . absolutely nothing else on underneath— you could see that. And a pair of mammaries! Mm!

FERGUSON *tensely:* Pete! I want to do some reading. Will you get the hell out?

PETE *sits up, looks at Ferguson, rises quickly:* Sure! *With a puzzled, backward glance at Ferguson, he goes. Ferguson switches off the radio; walks up and down the room, almost frantic, then throws himself face down, on the bed. There is a timid little knock at the door.*

FERGUSON: Come in! *The knock is repeated. Ferguson rises, calling impatiently:* Come in. Come in! *Barbara opens the door and slips in, breathless with the adventure.* What . . . er?

BARBARA: I came down for those notes . . .

FERGUSON: Oh! Of course. I forgot . . . stupid of me. Let's see—what was it? Materia Medica?

BARBARA: Yes.

FERGUSON *looks through drawer in his desk:* I had them here some place.

BARBARA: I suppose I oughtn't to have come in.

FERGUSON *assorting notes:* Pathology, Histology—no— no.

BARBARA: I hope nobody saw me.

FERGUSON: Materia Medica. Here! *He takes a notebook out of the drawer, glances through it, hands it to her.* There you are!

BARBARA: Thanks!

FERGUSON: Not at all! . . . Hope they're some help. *He goes to the window, looks out—dismissing her. Still in his old mood.*

BARBARA *stands there a moment, waiting. Finally she asks timidly:* Is there . . . anything wrong?

FERGUSON: What?

BARBARA: Anything wrong?

FERGUSON: Oh! No! No! *He turns to the window again. Barbara hesitates a moment—sees that he has already forgotten her in the intensity of his mood. She slowly turns, opens the door, looks out, and suddenly shuts it with an exclamation of fright.* What——

BARBARA *breathless . . . frightened:* Head-nurse! Outside!

FERGUSON: See you? Wait a minute! She'll be gone! Better sit down!

BARBARA: Thanks! *She watches him a moment.* Are you sure Doctor Cunningham didn't—— *Ferguson shakes his head.* Because . . . if it would mean anything . . . I'd go right down and tell them all—everybody—just what happened. . . .

FERGUSON: No, it's not Cunningham——

BARBARA: What is it, then?

FERGUSON: It's just—— *With an effort he shakes off his mood.* Don't mind me, tonight.

BARBARA: You work very hard, don't you?

FERGUSON *almost savagely:* Work? Sure! What else is

there but *work*—and *work! He suddenly realizes Barbara is staring at him. He pulls himself together.* Let's see those notes! *She brings them to him. He places the book on the desk, leans over it, and turns the pages.* There! *Barbara is next to him, leaning over the notes, her head near his.* These pages synopsize the whole business. Read through the notes carefully; memorize these pages—and you've got it! I think you'll find it lots easier that way.

BARBARA *pointing to a word:* What's this?

FERGUSON: Calomel!

BARBARA *her head almost touching his:* Oh, of course! It's a C.

FERGUSON *hands her the book:* Clear?

BARBARA: Yes. *As she reaches for the book, her hand meets his, and she clings to it.* You know, when I thought Dots was going to die . . . I got the feeling like I . . . I . . . God! . . . I can't put it into words!

FERGUSON: I know. I know that feeling. . . .

BARBARA: You, too?

FERGUSON: Me, too? *Clutching his throat:* Up to here, Barbara! Right now! Christ! I'm tired of work, and blood and sweat and pain! And the chap in 341 is dead! And Levine's wife is going to die . . . and one begins to wonder where in Heaven's God, and what in Hell's it all about, and why on earth does anything make any difference.

BARBARA *clutches his arm with her hand:* Yes, that's the feeling . . . and you get so lonely . . . and you feel . . .

tomorrow it's me . . . and the only thing that matters is just being alive . . . just being alive. Now! . . . Isn't it? *She is very close to George now, clutching his arm with her hand.*

FERGUSON *looks at her sympathetically:* You kids have a pretty tough time of it, don't you? Grind all day and lights out at ten o'clock.

BARBARA: And only one night out till twelve-thirty . . . and I haven't taken mine in two months. There's just nobody. . . . *They are very close, now. She almost whispers the last words to him.*

FERGUSON: You're a sweet girl, Barbara. *Suddenly he takes her in his arms and kisses her. She clings to him for a moment. Then they separate. He is confused and upset.* I'm sorry, Barbara . . . I. . . . *He goes to the notes, opens them—after a pause:* These diagrams here go with this page. Aside from that, I guess they'll be pretty clear. *He gives the book to her . . . grips her shoulder.* Please don't feel that I . . . just. . . .

BARBARA: Oh! No! No!

FERGUSON: Thanks. *Goes to the door . . . opens it . . . looks out.* I'm going up to Ward C, to look around for a few seconds. The coast is clear—you'd better go now. *Exit Ferguson.*

BARBARA *takes up the notes . . . walks slowly to the door . . . hesitates there a moment . . . is about to go out, suddenly stops . . . decides to stay. For a moment she leans against the door, breathless, then she goes back into the room, slowly drops the notes on the table, goes to the bed, sits down, takes off her cap, throws it on the bed and sits there . . . waiting.*

CURTAIN

ACT TWO

Three months later

Scene 1

A SOFTLY *lit room, the main feature of which is a long table. Seated about it are the members of the Joint Committee—three laymen representing the Lay board, and four Doctors representing the Medical board. Beyond them, we see mahogany panels, a huge fire-place and an oil portrait hanging over it, dark plush portières drawn to conceal windows and doors—in effect, a rich board-room of the same general conspiratorial appearance as the board-room of a railroad, a steel, oil, banking or other big business institution.*

AT RISE:

Mr. Houghton, short, stodgy, aggressive . . . the economist, has just finished reading a report.

MR. HOUGHTON: . . . 28,000—19,000—33,500 which adds up to a total deficit of 163,000 dollars so far, Doctors. *He shakes his head.* You'll have to cut down those expenses, Doctors.

DR. GORDON: How?

DR. WREN: We're to the bone, already. We've cut——

MR. SPENCER *presiding, gray templed, sure, suave, six generations of Harvard! He gives Dr. Wren the floor:* Dr. Wren!

DR. WREN *rises:* Everything—our staff, nurses, technicians, salaries, meals—telephones even! Our internes are allowed only two outside calls. . . .

DR. HOCHBERG: An absurd economy!

MR. HOUGHTON *taking some papers out of his briefcase:* Mm! . . . It seems to me we've a lot of people in our laboratories. Couldn't we reduce——

DR. HOCHBERG: No, no—— *To the chairman:* Mr. Spencer!

MR. SPENCER *giving Hochberg the floor:* Doctor Hochberg.

DR. HOCHBERG *rises, and explains, very patiently:* Those laboratories, Mr. Houghton, *are* the hospital. Most of our *real* work is done in them. *He smiles and shakes his head.* Without that pathology lab and the chemistry lab and the X-ray lab we're helpless.

MR. RUMMOND (*rather old and dim-witted, trying very hard to be a constructive part of this business, but not quite able to grasp it*): You are? . . . Really?

DR. HOCHBERG: Absolutely.

MR. RUMMOND: Hm. Interesting. I didn't realize they were that important.

DR. HOCHBERG: Oh, yes.

DR. GORDON: I should say so.

MR. HOUGHTON: Well, then. . . . *He looks at his papers, and shakes his head.* I don't know. 163,000 dollars—these days! The Board of Trustees is——

MR. SPENCER: Er. . . . We'll come back to that later, Mr. Houghton. I want to clear away all . . . er . . . Dr. Gordon! Any reports from the Medical Board to this joint committee?

DR. GORDON: Appointments! Two-year interneships, gentlemen—recommended on the basis of competitive examinations. *Starts looking through some papers for the list.* Internes. . . . Ah yes. *Finds his list and reads from it.* Aubert, Dickinson, Flickers, Frankey, Gordon, Kern, Monroe! The Medical Board awaits your approval of these men.

MR. HOUGHTON *quickly:* Where's Ten Eyck?

MR. SPENCER: You still can't do anything for Ten Eyck?

DR. GORDON: Ten Eyck? *He glances over his lists, murmuring:* Ten Eyck, Ten Eyck, Ten Eyck. Oh, yes—here it is. Gentlemen! Charles Arthur Ten Eyck finished fourth from the bottom——on a list of three hundred men examined.

MR. HOUGHTON: Senator Ten Eyck's going to be sore as hell. . . .

DR. LARROW *pompous pedant, cut pretty much from the same pattern as Dr. Cunningham:* I met the boy. Seems well-bred. Good family. . . .

DR. WREN: He doesn't *know* anything. I gave him his oral in medicine. An ignoramus.

DR. LARROW: Examinations! Bah! He graduated at an approved medical school, didn't he?

DR. WREN: How he managed it is a mystery to me.

DR. GORDON: We gave him special consideration, Mr. Spencer. But he just won't do. *Together*

MR. SPENCER: Well—his uncle's kicking up a fuss, but if the boy's that bad. . . . After all you know best. The appointments are in your hands. Which brings me to the real purpose of this special meeting. *He organizes his papers, clears his throat, and looks at them a moment. Then portentously:* Mr. Houghton has just . . . er . . . read the bad news.

DR. WREN: We usually run up a much larger deficit.

MR. SPENCER *smiles at this naiveté, so typical of the doctor in business:* Yes . . . but these are unusual times, Doctor. As you, no doubt, have heard, there has been a depression.

DR. GORDON: *Has* been? I like that. You try and collect some of my bills.

DR. LARROW: Yes. People are too poor to get sick these days.

DR. HOCHBERG: That's something no matter how poor a man is he can always get—sick!

Gordon and Wren enjoy a laugh at Larrow's discomfiture.

MR. SPENCER: Er . . . Doctors! Please! This is a very important matter! *They quiet down, and lean forward. There is no escaping the note of impending ill news in*

Spencer's manner. Two of our Trustees are very shaky, and may not be able to meet their usual subscription at all. They've already spoken to me about resigning. *The doctors look at each other. This is bad.* And so, I've been looking around carefully for a new Trustee—and believe me, Doctors, it was a mighty hard search. But, finally— *He smiles.* I found someone to underwrite our deficit. *Sighs of relief and approval from the doctors.* A man well known for his philanthropies, his generous soul, his civic and social services—John Hudson—the real estate Hudson. *Hochberg grunts.* A friend of yours, I believe, Doctor!

DR. HOCHBERG: Yes. But I didn't recognize him by the description. *Mr. Spencer laughs.* He'll be useful. The only real estate man I heard of who's made money the last few years. Good business head. He'll put St. George's on a paying basis.

MR. SPENCER *laughs:* If he can do that, he's a wizard. Mr. Houghton will resign in favor of him tomorrow.

MR. HOUGHTON: With pleasure.

MR. SPENCER: I've talked the matter over with him, and he's definitely interested.

Chorus of approval from the Committee.

MR. HOUGHTON: If we can get him to subscribe for. . . .

MR. SPENCER: Mr. Houghton! Please!

MR. HOUGHTON: Sorry!

MR. SPENCER: Now, it happens that one of our internes

is marrying John Hudson's daughter—in a few weeks, I believe. Of course, Doctors, appointments lie completely in your hands, but we feel here is an opportunity. We suggest the medical-board offer Dr. Ferguson an associateship. . . .

DR. HOCHBERG: What? Impossible!

MR. SPENCER: Impossible? A serious student, capable, going to study a year abroad under a well-known man—why impossible?

DR. HOCHBERG: He won't be *ready* for the job!

MR. SPENCER: Have you any personal prejudice against the boy?

DR. HOCHBERG *annoyed:* No . . . no! *He rises.* As a matter of fact I'm very fond of that boy. I think he has promise of becoming a good surgeon, some day. But not over night. He has years of intensive study ahead of him. I don't care what strength of character is native to a man—he will not work for something he can get for nothing—and Ferguson's no exception. An associateship here now simply means he'll go into practice and drop his studies.

DR. LARROW: And why shouldn't he? He's marrying well. . . . With his wife's connections, he ought to . . . er . . . do very nicely.

DR. HOCHBERG: If he doesn't continue his studies, he'll never be worth a damn as far as medicine goes.

MR. SPENCER: After all, Doctor Hochberg, that's *his* concern, not ours.

DR. LARROW: Oh! *Dubiously:* He's all right.
... But *with conviction:* he's no infant Cushing [1] by any means.   }*Together.*
MR. SPENCER: We must think of the hos-
pital, doctors! That's our job.

DR. HOCHBERG *losing his temper. To Dr. Larrow:* You're
wrong, Doctor. That boy has *unusual* ability. Yes, yes—
another Cushing, perhaps! *Controls himself—to Mr.
Spencer quietly:* Exactly, Mr. Spencer! The hospital! Do
you realize the responsibility in precious human life that
lies in an associate's hands? Ferguson doesn't know
enough, yet; he's apt to make mistakes that will hurt
not only himself, but the integrity of St. George's Hospital.

MR. SPENCER: Oh, come now, Dr. Hochberg!

MR. HOUGHTON: Oh, for Christ's sake . . . . }
RUMMOND: Nothing to be thrown away so }*Together.*
lightly!

MR. SPENCER: What do you think, Dr. Wren?

DR. WREN *slowly:* Well . . . he won't be ready for it,
of course, but—er—we could see to it that he'd always
be covered by an older man!

DR. HOCHBERG: And give him nothing to do! Make a
figure-head of him. Fine! That's fine!

MR. HOUGHTON: What of it?

---

[1] Harvey Cushing (1869-   ): professor of surgery at the Johns Hopkins
and Harvard Universities—the most eminent brain surgeon in the world.

DR. GORDON: Of course, we don't exactly approve of the appointment, however . . . .

MR. HOUGHTON *exploding:* Approve! Approve!

MR. SPENCER *irritably:* Mr. Houghton! Please! *Houghton subsides with a grunt.* Dr. Gordon! Go on!

DR. GORDON: Of course, we don't exactly approve the appointment for such a young man; however, we do need Hudson. And Ferguson's not a fool, by any means.

MR. SPENCER: Exactly, Dr. Gordon.

DR. HOCHBERG: But, Josh, don't you see——?

DR. GORDON: Leo, we've got to face the facts. There's hardly a hospital in this city that hasn't shut down on its charity wards. I know a dozen that have completely closed off entire floors and wings! If we have to economize any more, our wealthy patients will take care of themselves, but who's going to take care of all your charity cases? The wards upstairs are full, right now.

MR. HOUGHTON: It takes money to run a hospital, doctor! ⎱ *Together.*

DR. HOCHBERG *to Gordon:* You're right, Josh⎰
. . . you're . . . *To Houghton:* I know, Mr. Houghton, I know. And, believe me, we're deeply grateful to you gentlemen for your help.

MR. RUMMOND: A good cause. ⎫
⎬ *Together.*
MR. SPENCER: I only wish I could subscribe⎭
more, Doctor! I would.

DR. HOCHBERG: Yes. Deeply grateful. . . . Although, it's

a social crime, gentlemen, that hospitals should depend on the charity of a few individuals.

The Trustees look at each other, not quite sure whether they've been attacked or flattered.

DR. LARROW: The fact remains that we can't afford to refuse Hudson's help.

DR. HOCHBERG: I don't say that.

DR. LARROW: We need him.

DR. HOCHBERG: We do. And till hospitals are subsidized by the community and run by men in medicine, we'll continue to need our wealthy friends. I realize that. I say by all means make Hudson a Trustee. Take all the help he can give. And promise Ferguson an associateship as soon as he's *ready* to go into practice.

SPENCER: And that'll be—when?

DR. HOCHBERG: In five or six years.

MR. HOUGHTON: Oh, for Christ's sake! You're dealing with a business man there, not a child!

MR. RUMMOND: You can't expect the man to——

> *Together.*

MR. SPENCER *smiling wryly:* I'm very much afraid Hudson will tell us to come around ourselves in five or six years.

HOCHBERG *to Spencer:* How do you know?

MR. SPENCER: He wants the boy to open an office and settle down.

DR. HOCHBERG: He does? That's nice. Well, Ferguson won't be ready.

MR. SPENCER: If we don't appoint the boy we can't expect Hudson to be interested.

DR. WREN: There you are right, probably.

MR. SPENCER: Well, that's—er—the important thing, after all, isn't it? Hudson's interest.

MR. HOUGHTON: I should say it was his *capital! Houghton roars with laughter at his own quip.*

MR. SPENCER: Then you'll submit our recommendation to the medical board?

DR. WREN: Yes. And they'll O.K. it, too. I'm pretty sure it'll go through.

Dr. Hochberg throws up his hands.

MR. SPENCER: Fine! Fine! After all, Doctor Hochberg, as you say, we're here in a common cause—the hospital. *He smiles. Looks over his papers.* Mm! . . . Guess that's about all! *He glances around.* Anything else, gentlemen? Mr. Houghton? *Houghton gathers his papers, shakes his head "No", puts papers in portfolio.* Dr. Wren?

DR. WREN *looks at his watch:* No. Nothing!

MR. RUMMOND: What time have you there? *Compares watches, nods, rises, and gets his coat.*

MR. SPENCER: Anybody? Then the meeting is——

DR. GORDON: One second, Mr. Spencer! Since you're discussing this with Mr. Hudson, I think it would be a fine thing if we could extend our X-ray therapy department.

MR. SPENCER: First give him the associateship, then we'll talk about equipment.

DR. HOCHBERG *rises:* Don't count your chickens, Josh!

DR. GORDON: Oh, he'll get the appointment!

DR. HOCHBERG: Yes. But he won't accept it.

MR. SPENCER *smiles:* What makes you say that?

DR. HOCHBERG: I know the boy! He's too honest, too wise, to sacrifice his career for a nice office and an easy practice. Besides he won't have the time. He's going to work with me! And . . . er . . . well. . . . *He laughs.* It was perhaps a bit foolish to waste so much energy arguing the matter. *He starts for the door.*

MR. SPENCER *laughs:* As a matter of fact—I had dinner last night at the Hudsons' and I spoke to Ferguson about the appointment. He's delighted with the idea. . . .

DR. HOCHBERG *stops—returns—incredulous:* He said that?

MR. SPENCER: Certainly! And, why not? It's a fine opportunity for him. *Looks around.* Nothing else, gentlemen? No? . . . *Bangs his mallet on the table.* Meeting is adjourned!

All except Hochberg move toward the door. He stands there, stock-still, palpably hit.

BLACK OUT

Scene 2

THE *library.*

Dr. McCabe is sitting in arm chair reading. Michaelson is seated at the long table. Nearby Shorty is swinging an imaginary golf club.

SHORTY: My stance was all wrong, see? That's one reason I sliced so much. *McCabe looks up, grunts, and goes back to his book.*

MICHAELSON: I wouldn't even know how to hold a club any more.

SHORTY: You'd be surprised. A couple of games, and you're right back in form. Look at Ferguson! He hasn't played tennis in years—since high school, I think he said—and yet, last week he beat Laura two sets in a row. And that girl swings a mean racquet.

PETE *enters, sour-faced:* That patient in 310! Boy, I'd like to give him two dozen spinal taps and bite the point off the needle to make sure he feels them.

MICHAELSON: Whoa! *Laughs.* Your gall-bladder needs draining, Pete!

PETE: Ah! The smart alec! He invited me to share this special lunch with him. When I heard *lunch,* I accepted

*—he snaps his fingers—*like that! *Then, morosely*: Smart alec!

SHORTY: Well, what's the matter with that?

PETE: Do you know what 310's here for? *Shrilly:* Rectal feeding!

The others laugh.

MC CABE *looks up, annoyed:* Sh! Sh! Quiet!

They glance over at him and quiet down. He goes back to his books. They kid Pete in an undertone, muffling their laughter.

CUNNINGHAM *enters—looks around irritably:* Where's Ferguson?

SHORTY: Not here, doctor.

CUNNINGHAM: I've been trying to find him since twelve o'clock. What kind of house-service is this? Where is he?

MICHAELSON: Why, you see, doctor—Ferguson's being married next week, and he's at a ceremony rehearsal or something.

CUNNINGHAM: I told him not to let 327's bladder become distended.

MICHAELSON: 327? Ferguson catheterized him this morning.

CUNNINGHAM: Well, he needs another.

SHORTY: I'll get one of the juniors to do it, right away.

CUNNINGHAM: Never mind! I'll do it myself. *He goes to the door, grumbling.* Fine house-service you get around here. 327 is full of urine.

PETE: And so are you.

MC CABE *looks up:* What's that?

PETE: I'm sorry, doctor.

MC CABE: What for? You're quite right. He is. *The internes grin. McCabe looks at them quizzically. He turns to Shorty:* Young man! How would you treat the different forms of acute pancreatitis? [1]

SHORTY *a study in blankness:* Er . . . acute pancrea . . . mm. . . . . Why, the same way. I'd——

MC CABE: Wrong! *Pause, he shakes his head at Shorty.* You play golf, huh? *He tosses a pamphlet to Shorty.* Read that, and find out something about pancreatitis. *He suddenly draws his shoulders together and looks over at the windows.* There's a—— *He turns to Michaelson:* Will you see if that window's open? There's a draught in here, some place. *Michaelson crosses to the window.*

Through the glass-paned door, we see Ferguson in civilian clothes, and Laura coming up the corridor. They are in high spirits, joking and laughing. Ferguson starts to enter the library, but Laura hesitates in the doorway.

PETE: How was it?

FERGUSON *grinning:* Terrible.

MICHAELSON *to Ferguson and Laura:* Ho' there! *To McCabe:* They're all closed, Doctor.

FERGUSON *to Laura:* Come on in!

LAURA: Well—is it all right for me to——?

---

[1] Pancreatitis: inflammation of the pancreas.

The Internes assure her in chorus that it's quite all right. Ferguson takes her arm and pulls her into the room.

FERGUSON: Sure. Come on! *To others:* Any calls for me?

MICHAELSON: Yes. Quite a few, George.

LAURA: You should have seen my hero! He was scared to death.

FERGUSON: Who wouldn't be?

SHORTY: What was it like?

FERGUSON: Every step a major operation. Next time I take spinal anaesthesia first. *Shorty sings a funereal wedding march.* Exactly, Shorty! The last mile.

They laugh. McCabe looks up very much annoyed. He snorts, shuts his book with a bang. The others stop laughing and glance at him. McCabe reaches for his cane, rises rustily, and goes out mumbling.

LAURA, *watches him go, then turns to the others, who grin:* Perhaps I shouldn't have come in here.

SHORTY: Nonsense!

MAC: It's perfectly O.K.

PETE: Don't mind old Doc McCabe! He thinks the world ended in 1917 when he retired.

LAURA: Retired!

FERGUSON: Yes, but he still comes around to talk, read, watch operations. Gives us hell for not knowing anything. Medicine's not just his profession—it's his life. *He shakes his head admiringly.* Great guy! If I live to be eighty, that's the way I want to grow old!

LAURA: Not I. When I'm too old to enjoy life first hand I want to lie down, and say "Laura, it was good while it lasted. Now, *fini!*"

SHORTY: My idea exactly. Why sit around and listen to your arteries hardening?

PETE: Don't worry, sweetheart! The chances are none of us will live to grow that old. *To Laura:* Most doctors die pretty young, you know.

Laura looks pained.

MICHAELSON: That's right. The strain gets them around forty-five. Heart goes bad.

LAURA *glances at Ferguson and grimaces:* There's a pleasant thought.

FERGUSON *laughs:* Cheerful bunch!

PETE: So I say—eat, drink and be merry—for tomorrow you . . . *With a gesture:* Pht!

MICHAELSON: George! Better phone in! Cunningham's been looking for you!

FERGUSON: What's he want now?

SHORTY: His shoes shined, or something. I don't know.

PETE: 327 catheterized!

FERGUSON: Again? He'll wind up by —— (*goes to phone*) —giving that patient a urethritis.[1] *Picks up the phone.* Dr. Ferguson! I just came in. Any calls for me? Find him, will you? Library!

---

[1] Urethritis: inflammation of the urethra.

PETE: He's certainly been giving you all the dirty work lately.

MICHAELSON: Yes!

SHORTY: What'd you do? Kick his mother?

FERGUSON: What's the difference? Four more days and I'll be *aus* interne.

LAURA: Who is this charming fellow?

FERGUSON: He doesn't matter, darling! Nothing matters, now—except Vienna!

MICHAELSON: I bet you'll have a swell time over there.

FERGUSON: You bet right! *The phone rings. Ferguson goes to it. On phone:* Yes, Doctor Cunningham? ... Yes, Doctor Cunningham! ... Yes. ... Oh, you're quite right! ... Yes. ... Yes. ... *He winks at the boys, who smile and shake their heads.* Uh, huh! ... Yes ... yes. ... All right, Doctor! Sure.

MAC: Will you have lunch with us, Laura?

PETE: A lousy lunch.

LAURA *laughs:* Just had one, thanks! George and I dropped into Rumpelmayer's after the rehearsal!

SHORTY: Rumpelmayer? At the St. Moritz?

LAURA: Yes.

PETE *hungrily:* How was the food? Good?

LAURA: Delicious!

PETE: Oh? *Sighs enviously, then in a resigned tone:* Well—guess I'll go down and eat slop.

MAC: Sure we can't coax you?

LAURA: I'm full up to here! Thanks!

MAC: Sorry. So long.

Mac, Shorty and Pete go.

FERGUSON *still on the phone:* Yes. . . . Absolutely right, Doctor. I'll tend to it. *He hangs up, wrings the phone as if it were Cunningham's neck and grins at Laura.*

LAURA: Can I smoke in here?

FERGUSON: Sure.

LAURA *puts a cigarette in her mouth and waits for a light:* Well?

FERGUSON: What? *She points to her cigarette.* Oh! *He laughs, fishes out a packet of matches and lights her cigarette.*

LAURA: Darling! You're marvelous this way. I've never seen you so high.

FERGUSON: I've never been so high! You know, dear, I love this old place, and yet, my God, I can't wait to get out of here.

LAURA: I was worried last night, after Mr. Spencer spoke to you—you looked so glum. I was afraid you might change your mind.

FERGUSON: Not a chance!

LAURA: Not bothered about that appointment?

FERGUSON: No. That'll be all right—if I get it.

LAURA: You'll get it.

FERGUSON: What do you know about it?

LAURA: I know you, you fish!

FERGUSON *grins, then suddenly becomes serious:* I wonder if . . . Mr. Spencer spoke to the committee, yet?

LAURA: If he did, it's quick work.

FERGUSON: I hope he hasn't yet.

LAURA: Why?

FERGUSON: Well, I—want to talk to Dr. Hochberg first.

LAURA *laughs:* Why are you so afraid of Hocky? He won't bite you! Or, do you think by delaying it, you can change my mind—and work with Hocky when we come back?

FERGUSON: No, that's not it.

LAURA: Because if you do, I'm warning you! I'll just drop out of the picture, George. Even if we're married— you'll come home one day, and I just won't be there.

FERGUSON *takes her in his arms. Tenderly:* Shut up, will you? It's just that I don't want to seem ungrateful.

LAURA: Oh, he'll probably find somebody else.

FERGUSON: Of course he will. *Smiles, somewhat wistfully.* There isn't a man I know who wouldn't give a right eye for the chance to work with Dr. Hochberg. You don't realize it, dear, he's an important man. He . . . .

LAURA *impatiently:* The important man, George, is the man who knows how to live. I love Hocky, I think an awful lot of him. But, he's like my father. They have no outside interests at all. They're flat—they're colorless. They're not men—they're caricatures! Oh, don't become like them, George! Don't be an important man and crack up at forty-five. I want our lives together to be full and rich and beautiful! I want it so much.

FERGUSON *fervently:* Oh, my dear, so do I. . . . And believe me, that's the way it's going to be. *He looks at her fondly.* And I once thought I could live without you.

LAURA: What? When?

FERGUSON: Never! *He kisses her. Nurse Jamison enters, smiles embarrassed. Ferguson turns around, sees her, grins.* Yes?

NURSE: Mrs. D'Andrea—the mother of that boy—the automobile accident that came in this morning—she's outside, raising an awful rumpus. Wants to see you.

FERGUSON: Take her to Michaelson!

NURSE: I did! She wants to see you!

FERGUSON: There's nothing I can tell her now.

NURSE: I know, Doctor, but she insists on seeing you.

FERGUSON: What for? We won't know till tomorrow whether he'll live or die. *The Italian woman tries to enter. Nurse Jamison restrains her.* All right! Let her in, Jamison! Let her in!

ITALIAN WOMAN: Dottori. . . . Dottori. . . . Heeza all right? Yes? Heeza all right?

FERGUSON: I'm sorry! There's nothing I can tell you now.

ITALIAN WOMAN: Heeza gonna . . . live? Dottori?

FERGUSON: Tomorrow! Tomorrow! You come back tomorrow! We'll know then—tomorrow.

ITALIAN WOMAN: Tomorrow?

FERGUSON: Yes.

ITALIAN WOMAN: Mamma mia! Tomorrow! . . . Oh, Dottori! Pleeza! Pleeza! Don't let my boy die! Pleeza! . . .

FERGUSON: I'll do everything I can, mother. And you, try not to worry too much.

NURSE: Come! You'd better . . . .

ITALIAN WOMAN *to Nurse:* Oh, lady, heeza my boy. . . . *To Laura:* Heeza my boy! Heeza besta boy I got. Heeza besta boy in the world. If he's gonna die I'm gonna die, too. . . . *She prays in Italian.*

NURSE: Come! Come! *She leads out Italian woman.*

As they go to the door, Dr. Hochberg enters, passing them. He pauses to watch them go, then turns to Ferguson.

LAURA: Hello, Hocky!

DR. HOCHBERG: Hello, Laura! *To Ferguson:* Who was that?

FERGUSON: Mrs. D'Andrea, mother of that case . . . automobile accident . . . this morning.

DR. HOCHBERG: Oh, yes, yes, yes, I know—you gave him a shot of tetanus anti-toxin?

FERGUSON: Doctor Michaelson took care of that.

DR. HOCHBERG: He did? Good! *Glances at his watch.* Where have you been since twelve o'clock?

FERGUSON: I was gone a little longer than I expected to be.

LAURA: It was awfully important, Hocky.

DR. HOCHBERG: It must have been.

FERGUSON: I left Michaelson in charge to cover me. I only meant to be gone half an hour. . . .

DR. HOCHBERG: In the meantime it was two.

FERGUSON: Sorry, doctor! This won't happen again.

DR. HOCHBERG: I hope not. *He relaxes—becomes the old familiar again.* Watch it! A few more days to go. Your record is clean. Keep it that way! *There is a pause. Hochberg looks at George, steadily for a moment. George becomes self-conscious and uneasy. Finally Dr. Hochberg speaks:* George . . . I heard something this morning—I didn't know quite what to make of it. *Pause.* You still want to accomplish something in medicine?

FERGUSON: Certainly.

DR. HOCHBERG: You mean that?

FERGUSON: Yes.

DR. HOCHBERG *to Laura:* You love George, don't you, Laura?

LAURA: You know I do.

HOCHBERG: Of course you do and you want to help him —but that's not the way, Laura. Believe me, nobody can help George but himself—and hard work! He cannot buy this; he must earn it. *To Ferguson:* That appointment they talked to you about, George . . . you won't be ready for it. . . .

FERGUSON: After a year with Von Eiselsberg, I thought. . . .

HOCHBERG: One year? *He shakes his head.*

FERGUSON: It's not as if I were going to drop my studies. I intend to keep on.

Hochberg shakes his head.

LAURA: I don't see why not!

HOCHBERG *to Laura:* My dear child. . . .

LAURA: After all, George has worked so terribly hard till now, Hocky. If it's going to make things easier. . . .

HOCHBERG: There are no easy roads in medicine.

FERGUSON: I didn't expect it to be easy. I counted on work. Hard work!

DR. HOCHBERG: Ten years of it! Then . . . yes.

LAURA: I can't see how it's going to hurt George.

DR. HOCHBERG: There are a great many things you can't see, Laura.

LAURA: If he goes into practice, we'll have some time for ourselves, Hocky.

DR. HOCHBERG: Time? How? There are only twenty-four hours in a day. He's working with me and if—— *He suddenly stops short as the truth strikes him.* Or is he——? *To Ferguson:* Are you?

FERGUSON: Doctor Hochberg, I haven't loafed yet, and I don't intend to start now. But Laura and I are young, we love each other. I want a little *more* out of life than just my work. I don't think that's asking too much.

DR. HOCHBERG: I see. I see. *Pause.* So, you've decided not to come with me next year.

There's a long silence. Finally Laura answers apologetically.

LAURA: After all, Hocky, we feel that we'll be happier that way—and . . . .

DR. HOCHBERG: Of course, Laura. It's George's life and

yours. You've a right to decide for yourselves—what you're going to do with it. I didn't mean to meddle. . . .

LAURA: Oh, Hocky, you know we don't feel that way about you.

DR. HOCHBERG: I'm glad you don't. . . . *Pause. Trying to hide his hurt, he continues:* How's papa?

LAURA: So so. . . . He still has an occasional attack.

DR. HOCHBERG: Still smokes, I suppose.

LAURA *nods:* When I'm not around. He's building again.

DR. HOCHBERG: Well—don't let him work too hard!

LAURA: As if I have anything to say about that! You know dad! He usually has his way.

DR. HOCHBERG *glances at Ferguson, then nods significantly:* Yes. . . . *Dr. Hochberg turns to George and says gently:* You'd better get into your uniform, George. We may have to operate shortly. A new case just came in on the surgical service. One of our own nurses. What's her name——? That nice, little girl up in pediatrics? Oh yes—Dennin! Barbara Dennin! You remember her? Pediatrics.

FERGUSON *embarrassed:* Oh, yes, yes. I remember her—an excellent nurse.

DR. HOCHBERG: Poor child! Such a nice little girl, too. . . . Sepsis! [1]

---

[1] *Sepsis:* septic poisoning—the presence of various pathogenic organisms or their toxins in the blood or tissues.

FERGUSON *sympathetically:* Oh! That's awful! She bad?

DR. HOCHBERG: Temperature 105, blood count way up.

FERGUSON: Tch! What was it—ruptured appendix?

DR. HOCHBERG *shakes his head:* Septic abortion!

FERGUSON: Abortion?

DR. HOCHBERG: Yes. Poor girl—it's a shame. Well, we'll see what we can do. Meet me up there.

He starts towards the door. Ferguson stands there, his brow wrinkling.

MICHAELSON *entering:* That D'Andrea fellow is still unconscious. Seems to be something the matter with his lower jaw. . . .

DR. HOCHBERG: What!

MICHAELSON: Protruding—somewhat rigid. Thought it might be tetanus.

DR. HOCHBERG: No! Not so soon! Anyway, you gave him anti-toxin, didn't you?

MICHAELSON: Why—er. . . . *He shoots a quick glance at Ferguson.* No!

DR. HOCHBERG: What? *Angrily:* Don't you know yet that T.A.T.[1] is routine in this hospital?

---

[1] T. A. T.: Hospital jargon for tetanus-antitoxin.

Tetanus, the disease commonly known as "lockjaw," follows the contamination of a wound with dirt, which frequently contains tetanus bacilli. Antitoxin given shortly after such contamination is capable of preventing the disease. In most hospitals this antitoxin is administered routinely to all patients who sustain lacerations in automobile accidents, etc., where there is a chance of dirt gaining entrance into the wound.

MICHAELSON: Yes, sir. . . . But I thought—— *To Ferguson:* You didn't tell me. I thought you gave it!

DR. HOCHBERG *to Ferguson:* Doctor Ferguson!

FERGUSON: I intended to . . . mention it to him. I guess— I—forgot. . . .

DR. HOCHBERG: Forgot? Is that a thing to forget? You should have given the anti-toxin yourself!

LAURA: It's my fault, Hocky, I dragged him away—we were late.

DR. HOCHBERG: That's no excuse. He's not supposed to leave the house at all! And a very sick house, too. You know that, Dr. Ferguson!

FERGUSON: Yes, sir.

LAURA: Oh, Hocky—it was important! Terribly important! It was a rehearsal of our wedding.

DR. HOCHBERG: A rehearsal? Yes, Laura, that's nice. A rehearsal of your wedding. But, do you realize, upstairs, there is a boy all smashed to bits. There'll be no wedding for him, if he develops tetanus. *To Ferguson:* Doctor Ferguson! Inject that anti-toxin at once!

FERGUSON: Yes, sir! *He goes.*

DR. HOCHBERG *turns to Laura, looks at her a moment, then shakes his head and says slowly:* Laura, you deserve to be spanked! *Laura's face becomes angry and defiant. Her jaw tightens, but she says nothing.* Don't you realize what that boy's work means?

LAURA: Of course I do, Hocky.

DR. HOCHBERG *very softly, almost to himself:* No . . . no,

you don't! *Then, louder:* Would you like to see perhaps?

LAURA: Yes ... why not? ...

DR. HOCHBERG *glances toward the corridor where Michaelson is standing, talking to a nurse:* Doctor Michaelson! *Michaelson enters.* Take Miss Hudson here upstairs, see that she gets a cap and gown, and have her in the operating room in about—— (*With a sharp jerk of his arm he bares his wrist watch and looks at it.*) twenty minutes! *Without so much as another glance at Laura, he marches briskly out of the library.*

BLACK OUT

Scene 3

THE *end of the corridor. In the corner are the night-desk and a medicine cabinet. To the left of them is a room, numbered 401.*

To the right are the elevator doors. A woman and a boy are waiting for the elevator.

A nurse carrying a basin, some towels, etc., enters from the left. Mary comes out of 401, crosses to the night desk —takes a hypodermic needle and some bottles from the chest. The Nurse with the basin enters 401. The elevator whirs, and the doors open with a clang. An aged couple step out first, then Ferguson. The woman and the boy enter the elevator. The door clangs shut, and the elevator whirs. The aged couple cross to the left and disappear off. Ferguson starts to go into 401, stops, turns to Mary. Mary, who has been eyeing him, looks away.

FERGUSON: How is she? *Mary shakes her head. She is pale, grim, restrained.* Temperature?

MARY: 106.

FERGUSON: 106?

MARY: Yeah!

FERGUSON: Delirious?

MARY: She was—before—— *Pause, as she lights a small*

alcohol lamp, and sterilizes a hypodermic needle by boiling it in a spoon held over the flame. She kept calling—for you.

FERGUSON *suddenly rigid:* For me?

MARY: Yeah!

FERGUSON *stunned:* Oh! *He turns to enter the room.*

MARY: Better wait! Doctor Hochberg's in there. She's quiet, now. If you went in she might start talking again.

The Nurse with the basin and towels comes out of the room, sees Ferguson, smiles at him, and as she crosses left, throws a cheery hello to him over her shoulder. He doesn't answer. Nurse, puzzled, exits left.

FERGUSON: God! I never dreamed this would happen.

MARY: Men don't—usually. . . .

FERGUSON: Why didn't she come to me? Why didn't she tell me? Why did she keep away?

MARY: I guess that was my fault. Long time ago I saw she was falling for you. I told her you were in love with someone else, and engaged to be married—and to keep away from you. I didn't know then, that she already . . . .

FERGUSON: I see! I see! That's why she—I thought after that night . . . she'd just realized how crazy we'd both been. . . . Crazy! I thought she at least knew how to take care of herself. But when this happened . . . she should have told me! You should have told me! Why did you let her do this?

MARY: I didn't know . . . till last night. It was . . . too

late, then! She was just a green kid! Didn't realize what it was all about!

FERGUSON: God! I wouldn't have let this happen! I wouldn't have let this happen. . . .

MARY: I suppose you'd have helped her——

FERGUSON: Yes! Yes! Yes . . . rather than this. . . .

DR. HOCHBERG *pokes his head out the door of 401:* Where's that hypo?

MARY: In a second, Doctor!

HOCHBERG *to Ferguson:* Did you tend to D'Andrea?

FERGUSON: Yes, sir! Gave him the T.A.T. He's conscious, now.

HOCHBERG: That business with his jaw——?

FERGUSON *mechanically:* Slight dislocation. Put it back into place. Bandaged it! No further evidence of internal injury. . . . Although there may be a slight fracture of the tibia or the fibula of the left leg. I'll have some X-ray pictures taken this afternoon!

HOCHBERG: Uh huh! Pain?

FERGUSON: Complained of slight pain . . . general.

HOCHBERG: Did you give him some morphine?

FERGUSON: No, sir. . . .

HOCHBERG: Why not?

FERGUSON: Accident case! Didn't want to mask any possible internal injuries.

HOCHBERG: Ah! Yes. Very good, very good. *To Mary:* Er . . . tell me . . . was this Miss Dennin a friend of yours?

MARY: Yeah . . . in a way. I sort a . . . liked her.

HOCHBERG: Well, she's a mighty sick girl. You'd better notify her relatives. . . .

MARY: Ain't none . . . that would be interested.

HOCHBERG: No? Her friends, then? *Mary shakes her head.* My . . . my! *To Ferguson:* What a pity! Tch, tch! *He turns back into the room.* Oh, Wren, I want you to—— *He disappears into the room.*

MARY: Nobody! Nobody to turn to!

FERGUSON: Her folks? Her people? At home! Surely there's——

MARY: Yeah!—a stepfather! And to top it all, she's going to be kicked out of here!

FERGUSON: They wouldn't do that!

MARY: Wouldn't they, though? Ask Miss Hackett! And she won't get into any other hospital, either. They'll see to that!

FERGUSON: Poor kid!

MARY: It might be a lucky break for her if she just passed out!

FERGUSON: What are you talking about? She can't die! She's got to pull through! She's got to!

MARY: And then, what? . . . She hasn't got a dime to her name.

Hochberg and Wren come out of the room.

DR. HOCHBERG: Tch! Poor girl! . . . Why do they go to butchers like that?

DR. WREN: Well . . . she couldn't have come to us.

DR. HOCHBERG: No . . . that's the shame! Ah, Wren,

some of our laws belong to the Dark Ages! Why can't we help the poor and the ignorant? The others will always help themselves—law or no law.[1]

FERGUSON: What are your findings on the case, Doctor?

HOCHBERG: Definite evidence of sepsis. . . . Better order the operating room, at once! A hysterectomy![2]

FERGUSON: Don't you think operation is contra-indicated?

HOCHBERG: Not in this case.

FERGUSON: If we put her in Fowler's position and . . . .

HOCHBERG: You see, the infection is localized in the uterus . . . and it's been my experience in cases like this . . . the only way to save the patient is to remove the focus of infection.[3] Otherwise she hasn't a chance. . . .

FERGUSON: The girl was up in the children's ward. She

---

[1] Dr. Rongey, former president of the A. M. A., estimates that there are more illegal abortions every year in New York and Chicago than there are children actually born in those cities. Most of these operations are performed on otherwise respectable, law-abiding, married women. Proof enough that here is another social problem that can't be eliminated by legislation. No one wants to encourage the indiscriminate use of this grim practice. However, the lash of the law, instead of correcting the evil, only whips it into dark corners, creating a vicious class of criminal practitioner—bootleg doctors and ignorant midwives who work in dark, back-room apartments. A saner, healthier attitude is that adopted by the Soviet government, which is fostering birth control education, and instituting legal abortion clinics in a spirit best expressed by the motto inscribed over the door of one such clinic: "You are welcome this time, but we hope you will never have to come here again".

[2] Hysterectomy: removal of the uterus.

[3] Those who question this surgical procedure, see: Robinson, M. R.— Revaluation of the prevailing theories and principles of Puerperal Infection— *Am. Jour. of Surg.* 20:131:1933.

asked to be put there, because she loves them. It seems a terrible shame to deprive her of the chance of ever having any of her own.

HOCHBERG: It is. It is a terrible shame—yes. But, it's future life or her life. We'll save hers . . . if we can. Order the operating-room!

FERGUSON: Yes, sir.

HOCHBERG *to Mary:* And, the man, who—was responsible—— *Ferguson stiffens.* Does he realize what's happened?

MARY: I suppose so.

HOCHBERG: Mmm, hmm! . . . Who is the man?

MARY: I don't know!

HOCHBERG: Well—if you can find out he should be notified, at least. *To Ferguson:* What are you waiting for? Order the operating-room!

FERGUSON: Yes, sir. *He goes to the phone:* Operating-room! . . . Hello! . . . How soon can you have the O.R. ready for a hysterectomy? Dr. Hochberg! Yes. . . . *Turns to Hochberg:* Ready now.

HOCHBERG: Good! *To Mary:* Patient prepared?

MARY: Yes!

HOCHBERG: Fine! Er—give her that hypo!

MARY: Yes, sir! *Goes into Barbara's room.*

HOCHBERG *to Ferguson:* Have her brought up at once.

FERGUSON *into phone:* Patient ready! Send a rolling stretcher down to 401, at once! *He hangs up.*

HOCHBERG: Call the staff anaesthetist!

WREN: I'll give the anaesthesia, if you want me to, Hochberg.

HOCHBERG: There's no one I'd rather have.

WREN: General?

HOCHBERG: No—no. I'm afraid to give her ether. . . . We can work better under spinal anaesthesia.[1]

WREN: Spinal?—Good!

HOCHBERG: Come! I'd like to take a quick look at that D'Andrea boy.

WREN: I want to prepare my——

HOCHBERG: A second! Come. *To Ferguson:* You can start scrubbing, now. *Exit Hochberg and Wren.*

Ferguson stands there a moment. Mary comes out. She puts the alcohol and iodine back on the emergency shelf.

MARY: Well, that's——

---

[1] Anaesthesia: Ethyl ether and nitrous oxide, both intoxicants, were to the early part of the nineteenth century what rye, scotch and gin are to the twentieth. No hectic party was complete without an "ether frolic." An American dentist, noticing the numbness and insensibility to pain produced by "ether jag", applied the principle to the extraction of teeth. In 1846 he successfully demonstrated the simplicity and safety of ether in this type of minor operation. Before the year was up, ether was being used for many kinds of operation. "Shock" was now minimized, and speed became less important than good, neat, complete surgery. Then, for superficial operations, Halsted and Cushing, American surgeons, developed anaesthesia of a partial area by injecting solutions of cocaine into the tissue around that area. Another surgeon, J. L. Corning, introduced "spinal anaesthesia" by injecting cocaine derivatives into the spinal canal. This process gives the patient complete insensitivity to pain below the site of injection, without rendering him unconscious. The technique of spinal anaesthesia has been developed to a high degree and is now being used by many hospitals in preference to "general anaesthesia".

The elevator begins to whine. Mary and Ferguson glance over at the indicator dial over the elevator door. It slowly comes round from O.R. to 3, where it stops. The door opens with a clang. An Orderly steps out, backward, pulling a rolling stretcher after him. He turns to Mary and grins.

ORDERLY: Well, here I am, sweetheart!

MARY *suddenly bursts into tears:* Who the hell are you calling sweetheart? *She hurries into the room.*

ORDERLY *puzzled:* What the—— *He looks at Ferguson, embarrassed, smiles, and shakes his head in bewilderment. Then he wheels the stretcher into the room.*

THE ELEVATOR MAN *who has kept the elevator-door open, calls to Ferguson in a monotone:* Going down?

FERGUSON *slowly enters the elevator, then, in a low, harsh voice:* Up! Operating-room! *The door clangs shut, the elevator whines siren-like, rising to a crescendo, as the indicator dial goes up.*

BLACK OUT

Scene 4

THE *Operating-Room. A feeling of sharp, white gleaming cleanliness! Back center, the huge, hanging, kettle-drum lamp, with its hundreds of reflecting mirrors, throws a brilliant, shadowless light on the chromium operating table. All the nooks and corners of the room are rounded off to facilitate cleansing, and to prevent the accumulation of dust.*

To the right is the sterilizing room with its polished nickel auto-claves, bubbling and steaming.

To the left is a long North skylight, double paned.

There is one sterile nurse, wearing cap and gown, mask and long rubber gloves; there are two unsterile nurses, similarly clothed but wearing no gloves. They move to and fro like so many pistons, efficiently, quickly, quietly —ghost-like automata.

In the right-hand corner nearest us, stands a row of half a dozen sinks, the faucets in them turned on and off by means of knee-stirrups attached underneath. Above, a shelf holds cans of sterile brushes, pans of liquid soap, and eight-minute glasses—one to each sink. Well apart from these sinks, and to the right, are two basins in a white-enamel stand; one contains blue bichloride, the other alcohol. Beyond them again stands a foot-pedal gown drum, scarred from its purifying baths of steam.

To the left is a long glove table, on which are the gloves wrapped in canvas "books", sterile powder can, and towels covered by a sterile sheet.

Wren, in cap and mask, is dipping his hands in the bichloride pan; Pete, at the wash-basin, is cleaning his nails with an orange-stick, and Michaelson is scrubbing his hands with long, easy rhythmic strokes of the brush. They are chatting quietly.

The sterile nurse goes to the glove table and folds over the sheet, uncovering the glove books, etc.

A nurse comes from the sterilizing-room, carrying a steaming tray of instruments to the instrument table at the foot of the operating-table. The sterile nurse returns to the instrument table and there is a clink of instruments as she arranges them.

Wren holds up his hands so that the bichloride rolls down the forearm and off the elbow; he repeats this once more in the bichloride, and twice in the alcohol pan, then walks away, holding his dripping hands high and away from him.

A sterile nurse gives him a sterile towel. He dries his hands, using the separate sides and ends of the towel for each hand, then he tosses the towel to the floor, and crosses to the glove table.

An unsterile nurse quickly crosses, picks up the towel, and takes it away. Wren powders his hands, opens a glove *book, gingerly plucks out a glove, handling it by the cuff, careful not to touch the outside of the glove, as that might still soil it (since the hands themselves can never be completely sterilized) and slips it on. The second glove he slips on, careful not to touch his wrist with his already gloved hand. He then snaps the gloves over the cuffs of his jacket, wraps a sterile towel about his hands and walks over to the operating table.*

Pete finishes scrubbing, goes to the bichloride basin, and dips his hands, using the same technique as Wren. When he is through with the alcohol, however, he turns to the gown "drum". The sterile nurse crosses to the drum, steps on the pedal which raises the lid, and deftly extracts a folded gown, without touching the drum itself. She releases her foot, and the lid clunks back. She hands the folded gown to him; he takes a corner of it, unrolls it, and slips into it. An unsterile nurse comes up behind, careful not to touch him, and ties the gown for him.[1]

---

[1] Behind the fascinating ritual of this "sterile" or "aseptic" technique, which has the beat and the rhythm of some mechanical dance composition, lies the whole story of modern surgery and, indeed, the modern hospital.

Less than eighty years ago, hospitals were festering death-houses. It was far safer to be operated on in a private home than in a hospital, where the slightest surgical cases almost inevitably developed infection. So high was the fatality that surgeons began to discuss seriously the demolition of all hospitals.

Medicine pondered, "Where did infection spring from; and, how to combat it?" Dr. Oliver Wendell Holmes, appalled at the devastating mortality in child-birth, was one of the first to suggest that the physician himself might be the carrier of infection. Semmelweis, a Hungarian doctor, cleaned up his assistants' hands, and lo!—he transformed a Viennese delivery ward

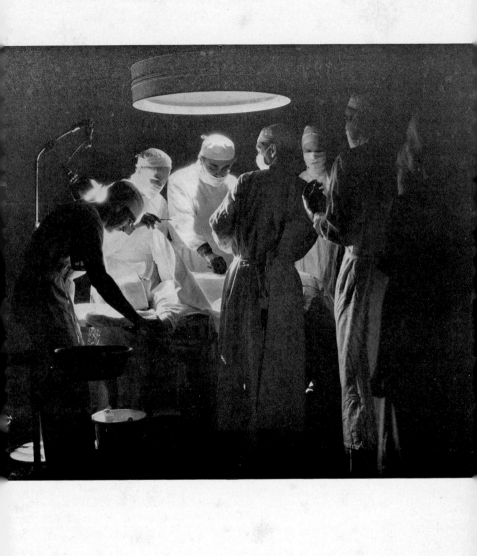

The whole effect is that of a smooth, well-oiled machine, a routine so studied that the people in the operating room can afford to be casual—as they are.

One of the unsterile nurses enters with Laura, whom she has just helped into a cap and gown.

NURSE: All right?

LAURA: Yes.

MICHAELSON *to Laura:* Well, you're all set, now!

LAURA *smiles nervously:* Yes—thanks!

MICHAELSON: Not at all! A pleasure!

LAURA *doubtfully:* Oh! The pleasure's all mine!

MICHAELSON *laughs:* I'll bet it is.

LAURA: This gown seems awfully wrinkled.

NURSE: They're never pressed. That would unsterilize them.

---

from a chamber of almost certain death to one of birth and hope. Then the Frenchman, Pasteur, looked through a microscope, and the whole course of medicine was changed. He saw the vast, invisible armies of microbes that ride the dust of the air, and realized they were the cause of decay and fermentation. But the great name in this story is that of Lister, the British surgeon, who took the torch from Pasteur and led surgery out of darkness into light. Realizing that infection of a wound was nothing more than a fermentation caused by Pasteur's tiny creatures, he sought about for a means of destroying these agents of destruction. He found a powerful weapon in carbolic acid. This was the beginning of "antisepsis" and a new epoch in surgery.

Gradually the "antiseptic" method was replaced by another which grew out of it. A technique evolved whereby instruments, dressings, gowns, gloves, etc., all steam-sterilized, precluded the necessity for powerful antiseptics, which often destroy human tissue as well as the enemy germs. No living bacteria are allowed near the wound. This gentler, if more elaborate technique is the "sterile" or "aseptic" one in use today.

LAURA: Oh! I see. *Enter Dr. Hochberg and Ferguson in operating pajamas. They are putting on their masks.* Hello!

HOCHBERG: Oh, hello! *To Ferguson:* We have a guest! *He turns over the eight-minute glass and begins to scrub up.*

FERGUSON *stands stock-still for a moment.* Laura! What? . . . .

LAURA: Surprise! *She starts to go toward George.*

HOCHBERG *warning her back with a quick gesture:* Uh, uh! *She stops.* Stand over there—in the corner! Don't come near us! We're getting clean! You're full of contamination.

LAURA: Oh—am I?

Ferguson begins to scrub up.

HOCHBERG: Yes. *A long pause while they scrub. Hochberg, still scrubbing, turns to Laura:* Well—how do you feel?

LAURA *trying to bluff off her nervousness:* Great!

HOCHBERG: Mm, hm!

LAURA: How do I look? *She holds out her gown at both sides.*

HOCHBERG: Very becoming!

LAURA: Think so, George?

FERGUSON: Yes—very!

HOCHBERG: You can look around, but keep out of the way! Don't touch anything! Put your hands behind your back! *A long silence, broken only by the rasping sound of scrubbing brushes. Laura stares, fascinated.*

HOCHBERG: Oh, nurse: *A nurse comes over.* See that Miss Hudson here gets a mask before she goes in. Find a stool for her—and put it near the operating table! I don't want her to miss anything!

LAURA *wryly:* Thanks, Hocky!

HOCHBERG: Don't mention it, Laura!

Dr. Hochberg finishes scrubbing, and goes through the same routine as the others. When he gets his gown he disappears to a corner of the operating-room, hidden by the basins. Ferguson, also, goes through the routine of gown and gloves, etc.

WREN: Orderly! Orderly!

ORDERLY *enters from anaesthesia-room:* Yes, sir?

WREN: Bring the patient in!

Barbara is wheeled in by the orderly. As she enters, Wren bends over to look at her. Ferguson comes over.

FERGUSON: How is she, Doctor?

BARBARA: George!

FERGUSON: Yes?

BARBARA: What are they going to do to me?

FERGUSON: There's nothing to be afraid of, Barbara!

BARBARA: You won't let them hurt me?

FERGUSON: No, of course not.

BARBARA: Will you be there? George, darling, please be there!

FERGUSON: I'll be there.

BARBARA: Thanks, dear. . . . I loved you. . . . I don't care. . . . *Her head goes back.*

WREN *looks at Ferguson, who is rigid. Then at Laura, who is equally rigid. He turns to orderly and says, sharply:* Come on! Come on!

The orderly wheels Barbara to the operating table. Wren follows. The patient is transferred to the operating table.

LAURA: What was that all about?

FERGUSON: Laura, I'm sorry as hell—I wish I. . . .

LAURA: George! Is it——? *She clutches his arm.*

FERGUSON *recoiling from her touch:* Don't! You mustn't! Stand away! Over there! You've unsterilized the gown! *He tears off his gown and gloves, throws them on the floor, and calls into the sterilizing-room:* Nurse! Nurse! Sterile gown, gloves, towels! Quick! *He turns to Laura, explains, apologetically:* We've got to be very careful. . . . You know . . . germs are . . .

A nurse enters, picks up the gown and gloves. He dips his hands into the bichloride pan, and then the alcohol pan. A sterile nurse brings him a sterile gown, he unfolds it and slides into it. And the sterile nurse, behind him, ties it. In the meantime another nurse returns with a sterile towel. He dries his hands, and throws the towel on the floor. The unsterile nurse picks it up and takes it away. The sterile nurse powders his hands, brings him a sterile glove book and opens it. He plucks out a glove, and puts it on, the nurse helping him, in approved aseptic tech-

*nique, by thrusting her fingers under the cuff, and push-
ing home the glove. In the meantime the patient, con-
cealed by the people around her, has been anaesthetized,
and is being draped. All the time Laura has been staring
at Ferguson. Ferguson, working the fingers of the gloves,
looks at Laura. Exit the orderly with the rolling stretcher.*

LAURA: Did you. . . . Did you have an affair with that
girl—or what?

FERGUSON *almost inaudibly:* Yes. . . .

LAURA: Oh! *A bitter little laugh.* That's a funny one!

DR. HOCHBERG *on a foot-stool, bends over the patient—
calls:* Dr. Ferguson . . . ! *The call is taken up by a number of voices. A nurse crosses to Ferguson.*

NURSE: Dr. Ferguson! The patient is draped and ready!

FERGUSON: All right! I'm coming! *He goes to the operating table.*

NURSE *to Laura:* If you want to watch—you'd better
go over. I'll get a stool for you—mask!

LAURA: No, thanks . . . ! I've had enough . . . ! I've
had enough!

A 2ND NURSE *enters* Here! Here! Get busy! *Notices
Laura.* You! What's the matter? You look so. . . . Feel
ill, dear? *To 1st Nurse:* Take her out! Near a window!
Give her some water!

LAURA: No . . . ! No . . . ! I'm . . . I'm fine . . . !
Thanks! *She tears off the tight cap, begins to sob, and
exits.*

The nurses look at each other and grin.

1ST NURSE: Med-student?

2ND NURSE: Of course! First time! What else?

1ST NURSE: She's got a long way to go, yet! *They laugh. Nurse and Doctors about the table turn and say, "Sh! Sh!" The nurses immediately hush.*

HOCHBERG: Ready, Dr. Wren?

WREN: All set!

HOCHBERG: Ready, Dr. Ferguson?

FERGUSON: Ready!

HOCHBERG *reaching out his hand, without looking up:* Scalpel!

The operating nurse hands over the scalpel, cutting a gleaming arc through the air, then she clumps it into Dr. Hochberg's hand. He bends over the patient. There is a sudden burst of activity and gleam of clamps about the table.

The unsterile nurses, hands behind their backs, stand on tip-toes, and crane their necks to see over the shoulders of the assistant.

All lights dim down, except the operating light, which bathes the tableau in a fierce, merciless, white brilliance.

CURTAIN

ACT THREE

FERGUSON'S *room. The next morning. The shade is drawn, the room dark, except for the small lamp at the bed. Ferguson is sitting on the bed, his head in his hands. His clothes are wrinkled—he hasn't changed them all night. His hair is mussed, his eyes red.*

A knock at the door.

Ferguson doesn't stir. The knock is repeated. Ferguson still remains motionless. The door slowly opens. Hochberg enters.

HOCHBERG: Good morning, George.

FERGUSON: Oh. Good morning. *Hochberg pulls up the shade. A great burst of sunlight streams in, blinding George. He turns his face away, rubs his eyes.* What time? *He picks up the clock.* Oh—I didn't know it was so late.

HOCHBERG: Lovely out, isn't it?

FERGUSON: Yes. . . . *He rises wearily, goes to the wash-basin, washes himself, and combs his hair.*

HOCHBERG *examining a brain in a jar on the desk:* Hm. . . . That's a fine specimen. Ah . . . yes . . . you've been doing some study on brain surgery?

FERGUSON: Yes. . . .

HOCHBERG: Fascinating work. Miss Dennin's temperature is down this morning. . . .

FERGUSON: I know.

HOCHBERG: The nurse tells me you watched the case all last night. That's very nice. . . . Hm. Excellent book—this. You should read all of Cushing's reports. How is er—D'Andrea?

FERGUSON: Examined those pictures. He did have a fracture of the tibia of the left leg. No further evidence of internal injury. He'll be all right, I guess.

HOCHBERG: Good. Good. He's a lucky boy. He looked badly hurt.

FERGUSON: Doctor Hochberg. There's something I've got to tell you. . . .

HOCHBERG *quickly:* I know. Wren told me. *Pause. Hochberg looks at the specimen:* Great field—brain surgery—for a young man.

FERGUSON: You must think it was pretty low of me.

HOCHBERG: George . . . George!

FERGUSON: I didn't know anything about it till yesterday. I wouldn't have let her. . . . I swear I wouldn't have. . . .

HOCHBERG: It was a bad job. . . .

FERGUSON: Oh, that poor kid. God, I ought to be shot.

HOCHBERG: Did you force her to have an affair with you; or did she come to you of her own free will? Then why do you blame yourself so?

FERGUSON: That has nothing to do with it.

HOCHBERG: That has everything to do with it!

FERGUSON: Dr. Hochberg, you don't know what she's up against.

HOCHBERG: I know.

FERGUSON: It's not as if she were just a tramp. . . . She's a fine, sensitive girl! God. What a mess I've gotten her into! She can't bear any children. Thrown out of the hospital—nowheres to go—no one to turn to. What's she going to do?

HOCHBERG: Don't worry. We'll find something for her.

FERGUSON: Just giving her a job—isn't going to help her very much. There's only one decent thing . . . I'm going to . . . marry her . . . if she'll have me.

HOCHBERG: George! Stop talking like an idiot! Pull yourself together! What about Laura?

FERGUSON: She's through with me, Dr. Hochberg.

HOCHBERG: She knows?

FERGUSON: Yes. I kept phoning her all day yesterday— all last night. She wouldn't come to the phone . . . wouldn't even talk to me, Dr. Hochberg.

HOCHBERG: Hm . . . that's too bad. Yet you know, George, in a way—that's not the worst that could have happened to you. . . .

FERGUSON: No! Don't say that!

HOCHBERG: Well, now there's work, my boy. Remember that's the master word—work.

FERGUSON: I'm going to marry that girl.

HOCHBERG: What for?

FERGUSON: I have to take care of her, don't I?

HOCHBERG: I see. You've saved some money then?

FERGUSON: Out of what?

HOCHBERG: Then how are you going to help her? How are you going to take care of her?

FERGUSON: I'm going into practice. . . .

HOCHBERG: Mid-Victorian idealism won't solve this problem, George. . . .

FERGUSON: That girl is human, isn't she? She needs me.

HOCHBERG: If you think you can provide for both of you by first starting practice—then you just don't know. . . .

FERGUSON: I'll manage somehow. I'm not afraid of that.

HOCHBERG: Remember Levine? I got a letter from him yesterday. Colorado. He's trying to build up a practice. . . . *The loud speaker in the corridor starts calling Dr. Hochberg.* They're starving, George. He begs me to lend him twenty dollars.

FERGUSON: I don't see what that has to do with me.

HOCHBERG: You didn't know him six years ago. He wouldn't *let* me help him, then. He was sure! So confident! And, better equipped for practice than you are.

FERGUSON: Possibly!

HOCHBERG: I won't answer for Levine . . . at least he loved Katherine. But you don't love this girl. It was an accident—and for that you want to ruin yourself—the rest of your life—destroy your ambition, your ideals—fill yourself with bitterness, live day and night with a woman who will grow to despise you. . . .

FERGUSON: Dr. Hochberg. Please—it's no use. I've thought of all that! It doesn't make any difference. There's only one decent thing to do—and I'm going to do it.

HOCHBERG *picks up the phone:* Yes? . . . Dr. Hochberg. . . . Yes, hello. . . . That's all right. Wait for me down in the—no. . . . Come up here to 106, 106. Yes. Is the man there at the desk? Yes. Hello, Arthur. Please ask one of the orderlies to show this young lady up to 106. Yes, thank you.

FERGUSON: Is that Laura?

HOCHBERG: Yes.

FERGUSON: I can't see her now! I can't talk to her.

HOCHBERG: Don't be a child! You've got to see her and have this out. *Pause.*

FERGUSON: Dr. Hochberg, I want you to know that . . . I appreciate all you've done for me.

HOCHBERG: What have I done?

FERGUSON: I mean yesterday. I . . . I must have seemed very ungrateful. But it's just because there are so many other things that I thought I wanted.

HOCHBERG: I know. It's our instinct to live, to enjoy ourselves. All of us.

FERGUSON: I love Laura so much. She's so full of life and fun, and all the things I've missed for so many years. I just didn't have the guts to give them up. I kidded myself that I could have that, and still go on. And last night, I realized I kidded myself out of the most important thing that ever happened to me, a chance to work with you. . . .

HOCHBERG: Do you still want to? You can, if you do.

FERGUSON: No—not now.

HOCHBERG: But why? If you realize, now, what you really want. . . .

FERGUSON: I'm going into practice, I told you. . . .

HOCHBERG: Now, George, calm down. Give yourself a chance to think it over.

FERGUSON: I've thought it over.

HOCHBERG: I warn you, George. You'll be sorry.

FERGUSON: I can't just ignore this!

HOCHBERG: In that case, you're through—you're finished—you're. . . .

FERGUSON: All right! Then I am. Why not? What good's a profession that can't give you bread and butter after you've sweated out ten years of your life on it? And if I can't make a go of practice, I'll find a job at something else—and to hell with medicine! I won't starve. I'll always make a living. . . .

Laura appears in the doorway accompanied by an orderly.

ORDERLY: Right here, Miss.

FERGUSON: Good morning, Laura.

LAURA *deliberately ignoring George, looking only at*

Hochberg, clipping every word: Hello, Hocky. . . . Did you want me up here?

HOCHBERG: Yes. Come in, Laura.

LAURA: Sorry to call you so early, but. . . .

HOCHBERG: It isn't early for me, Laura. . . . *She's still standing in the doorway, tense and hard. Impatiently:* Come in, come in. . . . *She wavers a moment, then enters.* Sit down.

LAURA: No. I'm in a hurry, Hocky. I just wanted to see you for a minute . . . alone.

HOCHBERG: Sit down, Laura.

LAURA: I suppose you wondered why I disappeared, yesterday.

HOCHBERG: No. . . . I heard all about it. . . .

LAURA: Oh, you did? A laugh, isn't it?

HOCHBERG: Not particularly.

LAURA: Well, you spanked me all right.

HOCHBERG: Harder than I meant, Laura. . . . Forgive me.

LAURA: Oh, that's all right. Better now than later, Hocky.

HOCHBERG: Will you please sit down, Laura? *Laura, suddenly limp, sits down. Hochberg, scrutinizing her face closely.* Sleep much last night?

LAURA: Sure. Why not? *She puts a cigarette into her mouth, searches for a match. George's hand automatically goes to his pocket, to find a match for her.* Light, Hocky? *Hochberg gives her a light. She exhales a huge puff of smoke.* I'm washed up with the whole business, Hocky.

HOCHBERG: Yes, of course you are . . . of course.

FERGUSON: I'm sorry you feel so bitter about it, Laura. . . .

LAURA: How did you expect me to feel?

FERGUSON: I don't blame you. I. . . .

LAURA: Thanks. That's sweet of you.

HOCHBERG: Neither do I blame him, Laura.

LAURA: There's no excuse for a thing like that—you know it, Hocky. None at all. . . .

HOCHBERG: I know nothing—except the human body, a little. And I haven't met the wise man or woman, Laura, whom impulse couldn't make a fool of. . . .

LAURA: If you want to reason that way, there isn't anything you couldn't justify.

HOCHBERG: I'm not trying to, Laura. It's so far beyond that. . . . *Ferguson starts for the door.* Where are you going?

FERGUSON: Upstairs.

HOCHBERG: Wait, George! Wait a minute!

FERGUSON: There's nothing more to be said, Dr. Hochberg. Laura's perfectly right.

LAURA *rises:* Don't leave on my account. I've got to go, now, anyway. I've got to pack. I'm sailing on the Olympic, tonight. Going to get as far away from all this as I can. *She laughs.* Humph! I was making plans. I was worried all the time. . . . God! What a fool I was. . . .

HOCHBERG: Do you think he's having such an easy time of it?

LAURA: Oh, he'll take care of himself.

HOCHBERG: Maybe you'd better go home now, Laura.

LAURA: I think it was a pretty rotten trick.

HOCHBERG: Stop it! Laura, stop it!

LAURA: He had no time for me—he was too busy for me—but he did find time to. . . . That's what hurts, Hocky! Hurts like the devil!

HOCHBERG: Don't you think I know how you feel, Laura?

The loud speaker is calling Dr. Hochberg.

LAURA: You think I still care? Well, I don't!

HOCHBERG: That's fine! Then it doesn't make any difference to you that right now he's throwing his life away. *Goes to the phone, picks it up, speaks into it.* Yes? Dr. Hochberg! *To Laura.* He's going to marry her, Laura.

LAURA: No?

FERGUSON: Dr. Hochberg! Please!

HOCHBERG: Yes. And go into practice, and starve and give up his studies and maybe get out of medicine altogether. The thing he's meant for! And worked so hard for. *Into the phone, suddenly tense.* Yes! What! Prepare a hypo of caffeine, and adrenalin, long needle! At once! *He hangs up and hurries to the door.*

FERGUSON: Do you want me——?

HOCHBERG: No . . . no . . . no. . . . You stay here! *He hurries out. Laura stands there a moment looking at George, then starts to go.*

FERGUSON: Laura!

LAURA: What?

FERGUSON: I don't want you to go away feeling like this. . . .

LAURA: What difference does it make how I feel?

FERGUSON: A great deal . . . to me.

LAURA *pause:* You love her, don't you?

FERGUSON: I love you, Laura.

LAURA *laughs bitterly:* Yes, I'm sure you do.

FERGUSON *grasps both of Laura's arms tightly:* I don't care whether you believe it or not, Laura, it just happens that I do.

LAURA: Let go—let go my arm! You're. . . .

FERGUSON: Sorry! *He turns from her and sinks down despondently on the bed.*

LAURA *after a pause:* Then how? I don't quite understand . . . I didn't sleep a wink last night, George. I was trying to figure this out. But it doesn't make sense . . . except that . . . I don't know. If you cared for me how could you do that?

FERGUSON: I don't know myself, Laura. Everything had gone wrong that day. Six long operations. I had a battle with Cunningham, I lost a patient. . . . Things sort of kept piling up till I thought I'd bust . . . this kid came to my room for some notes . . . she was sympathetic and lonely herself, and . . . well. . . . But after that I didn't see her around, and . . . I just forgot about it. You'd think she'd come to me when this happened. But, she didn't. I know I should have looked her up. I know I was pretty small and rotten. I thought . . . I thought it didn't mean very much to her. But it did, Laura! Now she's up against it, and. . . .

LAURA: If we meant anything at all to each other, you'd have come to me. I don't give a damn about ceremony! But the point is you didn't really care about me, George. Not for a minute.

FERGUSON: I wanted you more than anything else in the world that night, Laura. But we'd quarrelled and— you wouldn't even go out with me.

LAURA: It was that night?

FERGUSON: Yes.

LAURA: Oh!

FERGUSON: I didn't want to give up Hocky . . . and I didn't want to give you up . . . and I was fighting you . . . and. . . .

LAURA: Through her?

FERGUSON: Yes. . . .

LAURA *laughs bitterly:* And you say you loved me!

FERGUSON: If I hadn't, I'd have called quits then and there, Laura. I'd have gone to Vienna and worked my way through. That's what I was planning to do . . . before I met you. Alone in Vienna I'd really accomplish something. . . .

LAURA: Well, why don't you go on? Go on and do it, now. If it's so important to you. I won't be around to distract you! Go on! . . . But you're not, you see. You're going to marry a girl you say you don't care for. You're going to let a casual incident rob you of all the things you say are important.

FERGUSON: It's not a casual incident, *any more,* Laura.

LAURA: All right, make your beautiful gestures. Marry her!

FERGUSON: I'm going to.

LAURA: Go ahead! And inside of a year you'll be hating the sight of each other.

FERGUSON: That's a chance I'll have to take.

LAURA: You think you're being brave and strong, I suppose. But you're not. You're a coward. You're doing it because it's the easiest way out. Because you're afraid people'll say things about you. You have no backbone.

FERGUSON: Yes, Laura. You're right. I had no backbone when I let myself be talked out of a chance to work with Hocky. And maybe to do something fine some day. But right now I have no choice. I'm not doing this because I give a good God damn what anybody says or thinks; I'm doing it because that girl's life is smashed, and I'm responsible, and I want to try and help her pick up the pieces and put them together again. *He stops short. Laura is weeping quietly.* Oh, Laura . . . ! Don't!

LAURA: I knew how you felt about Hocky and I shouldn't have . . . insisted. I've been selfish, but it was only because I loved you so much. And . . . I still do. That's the way I am, George. I can't help it. I. . . .

Enter Hochberg, slowly, his face drawn and grave, something tragic written on it. He looks at Ferguson.

FERGUSON *sensing Hochberg's look:* What is it, Doctor?

HOCHBERG: Miss Dennin died.

FERGUSON *dazed:* What . . . ?

LAURA: Oh, God!

HOCHBERG: A few minutes ago.

Ferguson looks blankly at Dr. Hochberg, glances, as if for corroboration, at Laura, and suddenly starts for the door. Hochberg catches his arm and holds it tightly.

HOCHBERG *softly:* There's nothing you can do, George. Embolism! Went into collapse! Died instantly.

FERGUSON *almost inaudibly:* Oh! *He sinks down on the bed, his back to them.*

HOCHBERG: George!

LAURA: Darling!

FERGUSON: Only a few hours ago . . . she was pleading with me for a chance to live. . . . She was so young. She didn't want to die. . . .

LAURA: Stop it, George! Stop torturing yourself. Please! These things happen. It might have happened to anybody.

FERGUSON: Couldn't you do anything, Dr. Hochberg?

HOCHBERG: I tried . . . everything. Caffein intravenously. Adrenalin directly into the heart. Useless! That little blood-clot in the lung . . . and we're helpless. Forty years I've spent in medicine . . . and I couldn't help her.

FERGUSON: Then what's the use? What good is it all? Why go on? It takes everything from you and when you need it most it leaves you helpless. We don't know anything. . . . We're only guessing.

HOCHBERG: We've been doing a little work on embolism . . . getting some results. It's slow, though . . . slow. Maybe, some day, George. . . .

FERGUSON: Some day . . . ?

HOCHBERG: There isn't a man in medicine who hasn't said what you've said and meant it for a minute—all of us, George. And you're right. We are groping. We are guessing. But, at least our guesses today are closer than they were twenty years ago. And twenty years from now, they'll be still closer. That's what we're here for. Mm . . . there's so much to be done. And so little time in which to do it . . . that one life is never long enough. . . . *He sighs*. It's not easy for any of us. But in the end our reward is something richer than simply living. Maybe it's a kind of success that world out there can't measure . . . maybe it's a kind of glory, George. *Pause*. Yes, question as much as we will—when the test comes we know— don't we, George?

FERGUSON: Yes. . . .

HOCHBERG *goes slowly to the door, pauses there:* Er . . . we'll reduce that fracture at ten. Schedule the appendix at three . . . the gastric-ulcer immediately afterwards.

FERGUSON: Yes, sir.

Hochberg goes. Laura turns to Ferguson.

LAURA: Oh, darling! I'm so sorry! *Pause*. George, let's

get away from here. Let's go some place where we can talk this thing over quietly and sanely.

FERGUSON: No, Laura. This is where I belong!

LAURA: Yes. . . . *Pause.*

FERGUSON: You see. . . .

LAURA: I understand. . . . *Pause.* Well . . . when you come back from Vienna, if Hocky'll let you off for a night give me a ring! I'll be around. And, maybe some day we'll get together, anyway.

The loud speaker is heard calling: Dr. Ferguson!

LAURA *smiles wryly.* They're calling you.

FERGUSON: Yes.

LAURA: Work hard.

FERGUSON: So long, Laura. *Laura tears herself away, and hurries out. Ferguson stares after her till she disappears. The loud speaker calls him back. He goes to the phone, slowly, a bit stunned. He picks up the phone.* Yes? Dr. Ferguson! . . . Who? . . . Oh, Mrs. D'Andrea? Sure! Your boy's all right! Yes. Now, you mustn't cry, Mother! You mustn't! He's all right! *With his free hand he is brushing the tears from his own eyes and nose, for he is beginning to weep himself. But you could never tell it by his voice, which is strong with professional reassurance.* We'll fix his leg this morning, and he'll be home in a week. Yes . . . he's going to live . . . don't cry!

He is still reassuring her as the curtain descends.

CURTAIN

THE END

CAST OF CHARACTERS

This play was first presented by the Group Theatre and Sidney Harmon & James R. Ullman at the Broadhurst Theater on the evening of September twenty-sixth, 1933, with the following cast:

DR. GORDON	*Luther Adler*
DR. HOCHBERG	*J. Edward Bromberg*
DR. MICHAELSON	*William Challee*
DR. VITALE	*Herbert Ratner*
DR. MC CABE	*Grover Burgess*
DR. FERGUSON	*Alexander Kirkland*
DR. WREN	*Sanford Meisner*
DR. OTIS (SHORTY)	*Bob Lewis*
DR. LEVINE	*Morris Carnovsky*
DR. BRADLEY (PETE)	*Walter Coy*
DR. CRAWFORD (MAC)	*Alan Baxter*
NURSE JAMISON	*Eunice Stoddard*
MR. HUDSON	*Art Smith*
JAMES MOONEY	*Gerrit Kraber*
LAURA HUDSON	*Margaret Barker*
MR. SMITH	*Sanford Meisner*
MRS. SMITH	*Ruth Nelson*

DOROTHY SMITH	*Mab Maynard*
BARBARA DENNIN (STUDENT NURSE)	*Phoebe Brand*
DR. CUNNINGHAM	*Russell Collins*
FIRST NURSE	*Paula Miller*
NURSE MARY RYAN	*Dorothy Patten*
ORDERLY	*Elia Kazan*
MR. HOUGHTON	*Clifford Odets*
MR. SPENCER	*Lewis Leverett*
MR. RUMMOND	*Gerrit Kraber*
MRS. D'ANDREA	*Mary Virginia Farmer*
SECOND NURSE	*Elena Karam*

The Production was directed by Lee Strasberg

The Settings were designed by Mordecai Gorelik